THE RED SOX
FANATIC

EDITED BY DAVID HORNE

THE LYONS PRESS
Guilford, Connecticut
An imprint of The Globe Pequot Press

The Lyons Press is an imprint of The Globe Pequot Press.

Designed by Linda R. Loiewski

Library of Congress Cataloging-in-Publication Data is available on file.

ISBN: 978-1-59921-099-5

Printed in the United States of America

10 9 8 7 6 5 4 3 2

CONTENTS

INTRODUCTION

This book celebrates the shared experience of millions, the pure and innocent devotion of an entire region, the lifelong passion of its inhabitants and expatriates alike, the source of a joy and heartbreak incomprehensible to those who have never been infected by it, however knowledgeable they may be about the child's game to which it pertains. It is about a phenomenon of spring in a land of ice and slush, where winter persists well into April, like an army of occupation. It is the product of the wonder and delight, when, mere months since the four o'clock dusks of December, the click of a turnstile admits a boy to a Narnia where it is always summer, where, surely, within the green, asymmetrical ramparts, the grass is lush and the breeze is mild, even in January.

Boston's is not the oldest tradition in baseball: Cincinnati's is thirty-five years older. But New England's has a timeless continuity. Of the eight National League teams in existence when the Boston Americans were formed, only five play in the same cities today. Of those, only one has occupied its present stadium half as long as the Red Sox have inhabited Fenway Park. An annual parade heralds the Reds Opening Day, and, however chilly the day or night, the team begins its season before the rest of baseball. But my wife, who has followed the Reds since the days of Vada Pinson and Bubbles Coleman, has watched the team play in three different stadiums. Crosley Field, with its natural grass, its leftfield terrace, its homeruns launched onto I-75, is a memory. In the 1970s, when the Reds produced some of the greatest sports teams ever in the Midwest, the Big Red Machine played in a concrete colossus where even the dirt was artificial. The infield consisted of four sliding pits surrounded by the ground cover of miniature golf, its outlines painted on the carpet like a Groucho Marx mustache.

The Red Sox, by contrast, have made Fenway Park their home for the last ninety-five seasons. In the depths of the Wilderness Years, between Ted Williams's retirement and the Impossible Dream when attendance was a fraction of the draw today, the team replaced the infield dirt with fresh gravel ten feet deep. Jim Rice, Carl Yastrzemski, and Ted Williams all nabbed caroms that ricocheted, like ping pong balls from the same Wall. Joe Wood, Lefty Grove and Jim Lonborg threw from the same mound. When Coco Crisp lunges to snare a drive headed for the gap, he leaps over turf once patrolled by Jimmy Piersall, Dom DiMaggio, and Tris Speaker.

When the tradition passes from one New England generation to another, father and son, grandfather and granddaughter sit beneath the same green girders, lionize the same icons, marvel at the same bright popcorn-white uniforms as their elders had when they were novices.

In my family, the tradition spread in reverse. My mother attended nursing school in Boston, but never developed a fondness for baseball. When, as a teenager, I was smitten, we followed the team together. I remember where I was in 1963 when Al Luplow dove into the bullpen and stole a home run from Dick Williams. It was a Thursday. I was in the kitchen. My mother and I were listening on the radio.

I lost my father when I was young. My mother said that, before I was born, he drove to big games in Boston and New York. Big games: that means 1946, when the Red Sox won the pennant running away; 1948, the year the Red Sox and Indians tied for the flag; 1949, when the Red Sox lost the pennant in the last game of the year. Did my dad watch the Sox bury the competition in '46? Did he see Denny Galehouse crash and burn in the 1948 playoff? Was he in Yankee Stadium the next year when Tommy Henrich drove his dagger through the Red Sox hopes? I would have asked him about every pitch.

An abundance of uncles and aunts passed the torch for him. My Uncle Vernon and Aunt Pearl surprised me with tickets to the July 4th doubleheader in 1958, and, together, we visited Fenway for the first time. The seats were the best I've ever had: a dozen rows right behind the home dugout. At the end of an inning, Ted Williams sprinted in from left field straight at me, growing larger and larger, until I could discern his every feature. He was no longer the Splendid Splinter, but still ruggedly handsome and every inch the Marine. Then he vanished into the dugout.

I had caught the Red Sox bug, if my hosts had not. In 1996, I took Aunt Pearl for her second visit to Fenway.

My uncle Irving became their successor. A gifted pitcher and a southpaw, he received an offer to join the New York Giants organization. Baseball salaries were modest then, and he chose an electrician's career instead. I attracted his ire one summer day, when, humbled by injuries, Ted Williams took batting practice for the first time in his career, but, instead of witnessing history, I stole glances at photos of such Red Sox mortals as Dick Gernert and Willard Nixon. After 1946, Irving waited twenty-one years for the Red Sox to win a pennant, then died on opening day 1967.

In Fenway, every game could be magical. In 1961, with the Red Sox deep in the second division, we saw them battle a team a few games from the cellar. With the score tied in the ninth, Pinky Higgins summoned the bullpen catcher to pinch hit. Myron Ginsburg took an age to cross the out-field, but when he finally stepped into the batter's box, his smooth, swift stroke lined a shot over second base as straight and true as a physics demonstration simplified for grade schoolers. Jackie Jensen barreled around third base, grimacing, arms pumping, and slid across the plate ahead of a throw that wasn't even close. In the din that followed, I was transported into an ecstasy that only a thirteen-year-old can experience. There are no meaningless games.

This book recalls some great and some bizarre moments in Red Sox history and offers the insights of some who, with poignancy and wit, evoke the euphoria and chagrin of generations devoted to the Olde Towne Team: the spectacular success of the young franchise; the perfidious dissolution of a dynasty; resurgence under Tom Yawkey; the great players; the great races; the devastation of reversals at the very brink of triumph; and decades of longing and despair rewarded, at last, by keeping faith with idiots.

THE RED SOX

FANATIC

THE IRRESISTIBLE ALLURE

Boston is not a life-or-death matter, but the Red Sox are.

MIKE BARNACLE

More so than the Bruins, who have copped the Stanley Cup on five occasions, or the Celtics, who dominated a decade as no sports team has before or since, the Red Sox are Boston's team. To the faithful, Fenway Park is their shrine.

ALAN E. FOULDS

From now on, we'll wear red stockings and I'm grabbing that name Red Sox.

JOHN I. TAYLOR, BOSTON PURITANS OWNER, 1907

Something Old, Something New, Something Borrowed, and Something Red

Between their founding in 1901 and 1906, the Red Sox were called variously the Pilgrims, the Puritans, the Americans, the Somersets, and the Plymouth Rocks. In 1907, Taylor became eager to apply the name of a celebrated franchise, the Boston Red Stockings, to his combatants. The Red Stockings were formed in Boston in 1871 by leading players from Cincinnati when the Queen City of the West was omitted from the newly founded National Association.

The Cincinnati Red Stockings had been established as the first professional baseball team in 1869, and the Cincinnati players brought their mascot with them when they moved operations east. The Boston Red Stockings had a spectacular record, winning four National Association championships during the league's five-year existence. Upon the formation of the National League and the admission of the Cincinnati Red Stockings to the professional circuit in 1876, the Boston Red Stockings became the Boston Red Caps. The Boston National League franchise became known as the Beaneaters beginning with the 1883 season, and, because of their manager's belief that red dye in stockings infected wounds, the Beaneaters entirely removed red from the uniforms in 1906. By 1907, the redless Beaneaters had become the Doves, and Taylor acted quickly to adopt the mascot and color of a champion, while both remained in disuse. Taylor used the abbreviated "Sox," rather than "Stockings," after the example of the Chicago franchise that had abandoned a decade of "White Stockings" in favor of the ever-so-modern "White Sox" in 1904. The Red Sox should not be confused with the St. Louis Red Stockings, the Cincinnati Redlegs, the Boston Reds, the Cincinnati Reds, the Cincinnati Outlaw Reds, the St. Louis Maroons, or the Worcester Ruby Legs.

. . . I know how the fans are. I've been there for 10 years now and I understand. You're playing in front of the most passionate fans that I've ever played in front of. They expect you to win.

TIM WAKEFIELD

It's old-time baseball as the fans
knew it.

JOE GIARDINO

Baseball was there always, an eternal game eternally stretched for the seventh inning, and when we paused for breath in the hay field, my grandfather's clear storytelling voice would bring Smokey Joe Wood together with Johnny Pesky, Cy Young and Tris Speaker together with Mel Parnell, eternal teammates on the shadowy All-Star team of a farmer's daydreams.

DONALD HALL

Immortal Numbers

The numbers of the Red Sox greats that the team has retired are displayed in Fenway. They are: number 9, Ted Williams; number 4, Joe Cronin; number 1, Bobby Doerr; number 8, Carl Yastrzemski; and number 27, Carlton Fisk. During the 2003 playoffs, a television announcer stated that the order in which the first four numbers were displayed (9-4-1-8) was ominous. The start of the 1918 World Series had been moved up to September because of security concerns caused by World War I. Game 1 was played on September 5. September 4, 1918 (9/4/18), then, was the day preceding the last Series the Red Sox won through 2003. The announcer suggested that a reminder that the last Red Sox world championship was so remote in time was an ill omen. The numbers remain in the same order, despite the announcer's forebodings. They must have doomed the Yankees the next year.

Irresistible Allure Trivia Question

The following Red Sox players all wore uniform numbers that have since been retired, because they were worn by other Red Sox players. What uniform numbers did each player wear?

Jackie Jensen • Ben Chapman • Ed Sadowski
•Eddie Bressoud • Bobby Doerr • Joe Foy
•Butch Hobson • Bernie Carbo • Pete Daley
•Birdie Tebbetts

Answer on page 14.

[T]he Wall and . . . a team that keeps trying to win by hitting everything out of sight and just out-bombarding everyone else in the league. . . . All this makes the Boston fans a little crazy. I'm sorry for them.

ROGER ANGELL

My wife's parents had a retreat on a far hill of Vermont without electricity or telephone. . . . We parked our car on the edge of the woods and . . . I would . . . tune in the Red Sox. . . . . [O]ne day the car battery wouldn't turn the starter over, and we were stranded. I must have been the only man in New England who, rather than lose touch with the Red Sox, marooned his family in a forest full of bears.

JOHN UPDIKE

Answer to Irresistible Allure Trivia Question

Jackie Jensen and Butch Hobson wore number 4, the number worn by Joe Cronin. Joe Foy, Eddie Bressoud, and Bernie Carbo wore Dobby Doerr's number 1. Catchers Ed Sadowski, Pete Daley, and Birdie Tebbetts all wore Carl Yastrzemski's number 8. Bobby Doerr wore the number 9 in 1937. Ben Chapman wore number 1 in 1937. Chapman wore number 9 in 1938, the year before Ted Williams joined the Red Sox. Williams took Chapman's place in the outfield and was assigned Chapman's old uniform number.

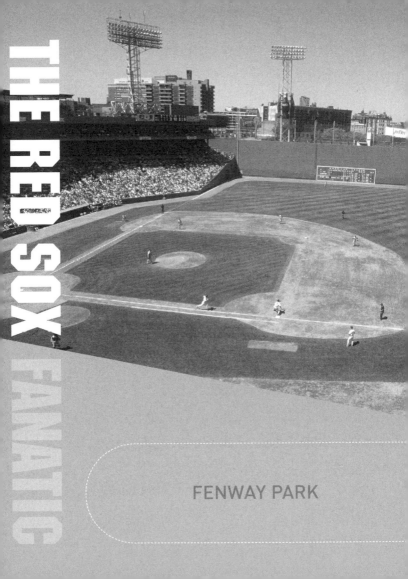

THE RED SOX FANATIC

FENWAY PARK

Fenway Park in Boston is a lyric
little bandbox of a park.

JOHN UPDIKE

A crazy-quilt violation of city planning principles, an irregular pile of architecture, a menace to marketing consultants, Fenway Park works. It works as a symbol of New England's pride, as a repository of evergreen hopes, as a tabernacle of lost innocence. It works as a place to watch baseball. . . . It's a ballpark, not a stadium.

MARTIN F. NOLAN

A friendly neighborhood joint, the corner bar of American sports palaces.

DAN SHAUGHNESSY

As I grew up, I knew that as a building [Fenway Park] was on the level of Mount Olympus, the Pyramid at Giza, the nation's capitol, the czar's Winter Palace, and the Louvre—except, of course that it is better than all those inconsequential places.

BART GIAMATTI

The Bijou of the East

TRADITIONAL ACCOLADE

Fenway Park Trivia Question 1

What stadium opened to major league baseball on the same day as Fenway Park?

Answer on page 25.

I've moved from the newest ballpark in the country [Miller Park, Milwaukee] to the oldest. It's the dream of my life. It's the best place in the world to be. Fenway Park.

DAVID MELLOR, FENWAY PARK GROUNDSKEEPER

Answer to Fenway Park Trivia Question 1

The first major league baseball game was scheduled to be played in Fenway Park on April 18, 1912. Two rainouts, however, delayed the park's major league debut until April 20, the same day that Detroit's Navin Field, later Tiger Stadium, opened. On April 20, the Red Sox beat the Highlanders 7–6 in eleven innings. This was not the first baseball game played in Fenway Park, however. The Red Sox played an exhibition game against the Harvard baseball team on April 9.

Love of Fenway itself may be as much a part of the Sox' 2.6 million annual attendance as Pedro, Manny and Nomar.

MICHAEL GEE

Every other stadium in the country you approach from a large parking lot with a huge façade. Here it's almost medieval. You come in off the street right into this dark, smelly warren of a lobby. It's great.

ANTHONY J. LUKAS

[O]nce you're there, you're rewarded by the timeless American pastoral of those men in whites spaced out in that meadow. It is a wonderful thing, like entering into an Easter egg. Suddenly after the hassles and traffic jam and getting in, you enter this world where peace and order is reigning.

JOHN UPDIKE

It's **never in** the past. This town, this ballpark are a part of me. I worked here. I give them my all. That's the bottom line. That will never change.

ROGER CLEMENS

Home-and-Home Series

Boston's Miracle Braves played their home games for the 1914 World Series in Fenway Park, because it was much larger than their South End Grounds. The Braves' success in that miracle year led their owner to construct Braves Field, which, at 40,000 seats, was a colossus by the standards of the time. When the Red Sox won the American League pennant in 1915 and 1916, they played their World Series home games in Braves Field because it had nearly 7,000 more seats than Fenway Park.

[M]ost of the parks [built] these days favor the left-handed hitters. Fenway was always right-handed, and it's always been one of the few.

BOBBY DOERR

I've always said that this is a
left-hand hitter's park.

CURT GOWDY

Fenway Park is not as much of a hitter's park as it once was, although it still favors the hitter more than the pitcher. As always, the park favors right-handed pitchers and power hitters, but left-handed high-average hitters.

BILL JAMES

James theorized that a pitcher cannot afford to throw outside to a left-handed hitter in Fenway Park, because he will hit the Monster à la Fred Lynn. Fed a diet of inside pitches, left-handed hitters get more pitches that they can see and hit. The statistics bear James out. James starts an analysis with statistics, identifies a fact or trend, and then suggests a theory to explain the undeniable.

Over the years its slugging percentage is greater than Ruth's, Gehrig's, Musial's and Aaron's put together. Roger Maris hit 61 home runs in a season? Pshaw! On its good streaks, The Wall had more than that in a month.

JIM MURRAY

Curt Gowdy and Bill James are correct in noting that Fenway Park favors left-handed hitters for batting average. Before the era of Nomar and Manny, all but 2 of the 21 batting crowns won by Red Sox players belonged to either left-handed hitters or switch hitters.

Dale Alexander	1932	.367	Right
Ted Williams	1941	.406	Left
Ted Williams	1942	.356	Left
Ted Williams	1947	.343	Left
Ted Williams	1948	.369	Left
Billy Goodman	1950	.354	Left
Ted Williams	1957	.388	Left
Ted Williams	1958	.328	Left
Pete Runnels	1960	.320	Left
Pete Runnels	1962	.326	Left
Carl Yastrzemski	1963	.321	Left
Carl Yastrzemski	1967	.326	Left
Carl Yastrzemski	1968	.301	Left

Reggie Smith	1969	.309	Both
Fred Lynn	1979	.333	Left
Carney Lansford	1981	.336	Right
Wade Boggs	1983	.361	Left
Wade Boggs	1985	.361	Left
Wade Boggs	1986	.357	Left
Wade Boggs	1987	.363	Left
Wade Boggs	1988	.366	Left
Nomar Garciaparra	1999	.357	Right
Nomar Garciaparra	2000	.372	Right
Manny Ramirez	2002	.349	Right
Bill Mueller	2003	.326	Both

The absence of batting champions from Fenway Park during its first twenty years is due largely to the monopolization of the crown by Detroit's Ty Cobb and Harry Heilmann and the dreadful Red Sox clubs of the 1920s, when Boston essentially served as a farm team for the Yankees.

Fenway Park Trivia Question 2

Red Sox players hold the single-season and career records for doubles. One player is in the Hall of Fame. The other is notable only for his record. Who are they, and how many doubles did each hit to set their records?

Answer on page 42.

The Red Sox often feed visitors to the Green Monster . . .

SKIP BAYLESS

[The Wall] has an effect on the
organization from top to bottom.

TOM YAWKEY

Do they leave it there during games?

BILL LEE, REFERRING TO THE WALL

Answer to Fenway Park Trivia
Question 2

Outfielder Earl Webb had an eight-year major league career. He played for the Red Sox from 1930 to 1932. Over his career, he hit 155 doubles. Other than 1931, his highest single season doubles total was 30. In 1931, one of two full seasons he played in Fenway Park, he hit 67 doubles, a record that stands today. Tris Speaker, the great Red Sox centerfielder of the second decade of the twentieth century, was inducted into the Hall of Fame in 1937. At the time of his retirement in 1928 he was in the top ten all-time in hits, triples, and runs scored. His mark of 792 career doubles remains the highest of all time. Doubles are a key element in the attack of successful Red Sox teams. The American League champion 1975 Red Sox led the league in doubles, hitting 21 more than the runner-up in that category. In commenting on the American League championship season of 1986, Bill James noted that the Red Sox hit more doubles that year than any team since the 1937 Cardinals.

Duffy's Cliff

Terraces have been used in several ballparks to serve the same purpose as a warning track. Crosley Field was the home of the Cincinnati Reds before Riverfront Stadium opened early in the 1970 season. A left-field terrace was one of its distinguishing features. The terrace in Houston's Minute Maid Park mimics those from ballparks of long ago. From its opening in 1912 through 1933, Fenway Park featured an outfield terrace that extended from the leftfield foul pole to the flag pole in centerfield and was steep enough to pose a challenge to outfielders chasing fly balls at full speed. Red Sox star leftfielder Duffy Lewis became particularly adept at playing the terrace, and it was dubbed "Duffy's Cliff."

They made a mountain goat out of me.

DUFFY LEWIS

If a guy's blind, he might not notice the fence.

PETE ROSE

The best thing they can do is tear it down.

GEORGE FOSTER, REFERRING TO THE WALL

You see that wall for the first time and you have a tendency to go for it and that's what the Boston pitchers want you to do.

TED KLUSZEWSKI

Browns Bomber

During a game between the Red Sox and the St. Louis Browns at Fenway Park on May 17, 1947, a seagull flew over the field and lost control of a three-pound smelt it was carrying in its beak. The fish plummeted to earth and landed on the pitcher's mound, narrowly missing Browns hurler Ellis Kinder.

I don't see how a left-hander could [win consistently in Fenway Park]. You have to keep every pitch down, and against the right-handers you can only use the outside part of the plate.

BILL MONBOUQUETTE

Fenway Park's most famous feature is its short left field, which makes peculiar demands of defenders. Less celebrated, but just as demanding, is the opposite field. . . . . Fenway's right field wall is like a hockey rink's—the corner is rounded and the ball will scoot over to center quickly. . . . . [I]f a player tries to cut the ball off and fails, it will be the last he sees of it.

FRED PERCIVAL

Fenway Park Trivia Question 3

Which of the following pitchers, all of whom were successful at Fenway Park, were left-handers? If some names are unfamiliar, it is because the list extends into the dead-ball era.

A.	Bill Lee
B.	Bruce Hurst
C.	Mel Parnell
D.	Mose Grove
E.	Jidge Ruth

Answer on page 55.

It is said in Boston that the sun rises in the east and sets in the eyes of the right fielder.

BRUCE NASH AND ALLAN ZULLO

I went there as a kid. You never knew what would happen—pop fly homers down the lines, a ball off the Wall. A guy could miss an inside-the-park homer. Nothing was uniform. Let me tell ya', that was the miracle of the place.

TIP O'NEILL

I don't know much about classical music, but if there's a baseball symphony, this is it.

BUCK SHOWALTER

Answer to Fenway Park Trivia Question 3

All are southpaws. Bill Lee won seventeen games each in 1973, 1974, and 1975. Bruce Hurst won thirteen games for the Red Sox in 1986 with a 2.99 ERA and won Games 2 and 5 in the 1986 World Series. He recorded fifteen victories in 1987 and eighteen in 1988. Mel Parnell is one of the greatest of Red Sox left-handers. He twice won eighteen games and once won twenty. In 1949, he led the American League with twenty-five wins, twenty-seven complete games, and 295 1/3 innings pitched. Mose Grove is Robert Moses Grove, better known as Lefty Grove, the greatest southpaw in the first one hundred years of Major League Baseball. Grove notched ninety-seven of his three hundred wins for Boston, including twenty in 1935, and led the league in earned run average four times as a Red Sox pitcher. Jidge was short for George, as in George Herman Ruth, more familiar as Babe Ruth. His talent as a pitcher has been justifiably called prodigious. He won twenty-three games for the Red Sox in 1916 with a league-leading ERA of 1.75, and twenty-four more games in 1917. In 1918, he set a record for consecutive scoreless innings in the World Series that stood until 1961. Ruth's achievements as the greatest slugger in baseball history and as a brilliant pitcher led Bob Costas to remark, "It's as if Beethoven and Cezanne were the same person."

Above and Beyond

On May 22, 1984, a Red Sox utility infielder achieved sports immortality. On that date, a rat appeared near the on-deck circle at Fenway Park during a game between the Red Sox and the Indians. The audacious rodent proceeded first toward the mound, then toward the third-base foul line. First baseman Ed Jurak, a career .238 hitter, darted across the infield, grabbed the rat in his glove, and disposed of it in a trash can in the Red Sox dugout, earning a place of eternal glory in the pantheon of sports trivia.

Jurak's place in the sun was ordained by fate. In the Chinese astrological calendar, 1984 was the Year of the Rat.

The Lonely Red Seat

One seat in Fenway is painted red. Seat 21 in Section 42, Row 37 in the rightfield bleachers stands out alone among the countless green seats. In 1946, Ted Williams hit a 502-foot home run off Detroit's Fred Hutchinson that landed on that seat. Actually, the ball hit the fan sitting in that seat on the head, but there is no credible evidence that the fan's head was painted to commemorate the occasion.

THE RED SOX

FANATIC

A GLORIOUS BEGINNING

1903

When the American League was formed in 1900, the upstarts raided the rosters of the National League mercilessly. Greats Napoleon Lajoie, John McGraw, Joe McGinnity, Clark Griffith, and "Turkey Mike" Donlin, veteran leaders Fielder Jones, Jack McCarthy, and John Anderson, and a good deal of restless young talent jumped leagues for the inaugural season. Stars such as Jack Chesbro, Bill Dineen, and Elmer Flick soon followed. The new Boston team signed all-around great and future Hall of Fame third baseman Jimmy Collins away from the National League's Boston Beaneaters and installed him as their player-manager.

Everything's fair in love, war and baseball.

JIMMY COLLINS

With a swoop like that of a chicken hawk, Collins would gather up the bunt and throw it accurately to whoever should receive it. The beauty about him was that he could throw from any angle, any position on the ground or in the air.

SPALDING GUIDE, 1902

The new Boston franchise, then called the "Somersets," grabbed a catcher with a strong throwing arm from the roster of the St. Louis Blues.

[Lou Criger] wasn't a great hitter by any means. . . . He had a low batting average, but Lou would drive in a lot of runs. And what a catcher. In eight years I never saw him drop a foul ball. Even Ty Cobb had all kinds of trouble running the bases on Lou.

FRED PARENT

The biggest plum for the fledgling franchise was the ace of the St. Louis Blues rotation, the rotund thirty-three-year-old right-hander who would win more games than any pitcher in major league history: Cy Young.

One of the fellows called me "Cyclone" but finally shortened it to "Cy" and its been that ever since.

CY YOUNG

Connie Mack, who has seen more ball games than any other American living or dead, always considered Young's perfect game against Rube Waddell in 1904 the greatest exhibition of pitching ever performed.

TOM MEANY

Young fared well in the new bush league, leading the circuit in earned run average in 1901, winning percentage in 1903 and, with 53 victories over his first three seasons, in wins for three years running. He won 235 games after jumping leagues, retiring with the astonishing total of 511. The award for the best pitcher in each league is named after Cy Young, because he won hundreds of games in both circuits.

Did you really play in the major leagues?

FAN TO CY YOUNG

Son, I won more games than you'll ever see.

CY YOUNG

For the first three years, the two leagues were openly hostile to each other.

The contract-breaking, the player-jumping from league to league, the bickering and the name-calling that took place in baseball's infancy soured the fans to such an extent that the attendance in both leagues suffered drastically.

JOSEPH L. REICHLER

In 1903, the Pirates, led by their immortal shortstop, the Flying Dutchman Honus Wagner, won the N.L. flag by six and a half games.

[Honus Wagner] was a gentle, kind man, a storyteller, supportive of rookies, patient with the fans, cheerful in hard times, careful of the example he set for youth, a hard worker, a man who had no enemies and who never forget his friends. He was the most beloved man in baseball before Ruth.

BILL JAMES

The new Boston franchise, now dubbed the "Pilgrims," won the pennant in the upstart league by fourteen and a half games. The owner of the National League champions conceived a way to defuse the tensions between the rival circuits.

The time has come for the National League and American League to organize a World Series. It is my belief that if our clubs played a series on a best-of-nine basis, we would create great interest in baseball, in our leagues, and in our players. I also believe it would be a financial success.

BARNEY DREYFUSS, PIRATES OWNER, IN A LETTER TO JOHN I. TAYLOR, PILGRIMS OWNER, AUGUST 1903

The World Series attracted a rabid following, at least initially.

In Boston the fans broke down the fence. And before it broke down some fans were pulling up others with ropes over that fence for $1 or $2 a head. What a way to run a World Series!

FRED PARENT, BOSTON SHORTSTOP

As the new World Series began, there was bravado on both sides.

Hey Dutchman, we're going to give you and the Pirates a good licking!

BOSTON FAN

Who with—that old man, Cy Young?

HONUS WAGNER

The Boston fans formed the Royal Rooters, a raucus group of diehards who appropriated their own section in the grandstands. They adopted the Broadway tune "Tessie" as the official ballad of the Boston Pilgrims. They frequently traveled as a group to key Pilgrims road games, carrying banners eight feet long. The Rooters sang "Tessie" in Pittsburgh during the 1903 World Series, accompanied by a large drum and noisemakers.

Tessie, you make me feel so badly.

> Why don't you turn around?
>
> Tessie you know I love you madly.
>
> Babe, my heart weighs about a pound.
>
> Don't blame me if I ever doubt you.
>
> You know I couldn't live without you.
>
> Tessie, you are my only, only, only.

WILL R. ANDERSON, FROM THE MUSICAL *THE SILVER SLIPPER*

The Royal Rooters adapted "Tessie" especially for Honus Wagner.

Honus, why do you hit so badly?

The Pilgrims' player-manager could not resist some ill-advised candor.

[T]he Pittsburgs do not look so strong to me. They show up strong because they are in a poorer league than the American.

JIMMY COLLINS

Collins's braggadocio must have inspired the Pirates. They took the first two games of the Series.

We just couldn't get started. We didn't get the breaks in these first four games. We were hitting the ball hard— and we were a hitting team—but it would go straight to someone, or one of the Pittsburgh players would come up with a sensational catch. . . . After we started getting the breaks we could have beaten them 50 games easy.

FRED PARENT

Song of the Half Century

It became traditional for the organist at Fenway Park to play "Tessie" at the Red Sox home opener every year through the mid-1960s. Boston hurlers Bill Dineen and Cy Young brought the Pilgrims back. Dineen won three games, throwing two shutouts, one of them in the deciding Game 8. Cy Young rebounded from a loss in Game 1 to complete game victories in Games 5 and 7, inspiring songs of praise.

Yes, it's rah! Cy, rah! from the
wide world's heart!
You're the pride of every fan, Cy!
You are prince and peer
Of the speeding sphere
And, besides, a clean square
man, Cy!

JAC LOWELL

So when a stalwart steps out
        from the throng,
On with the tribute, let garlands
        be flung—
Here's to the sturdy and here's to
        the strong
Here's to the king of them all;
        Denton Young

Grantland Rice

An Odd Division of the Spoils

Each winning player's share for the 1903 World Series was $1,182. Each losing player's share was $1,316. No, this isn't base fourteen arithmetic. Pittsburgh owner Barney Dreyfuss contributed his share of the World Series earnings to the players' pool. What the Pirates lost on the battlefield they won at the owner's table.

The Royal Rooters' taunting, along with the injury bug, did the Pirates in. The Flying Dutchman, less than 100 percent with a leg injury, hit only .222 in the World Series.

Didn't Cy and Bill make the Dutchman look good? National League batting champion my eye.

HOBE FERRIS, BOSTON SECOND BASEMAN

It's difficult to imagine a World Series that didn't rivet public attention for the duration. The *New York Times* article about the deciding game, however, found it necessary to emphasize the celebration of the Pilgrims fans to portray the inaugural championship series as a popular success.

The Boston Americans shut out the Pittsburg Nationals to-day and won the world's baseball championship, to the almost frenzied delight of 7,000 enthusiasts. While the attendance at all the previous games of the series has been larger than to-day, the demonstration which followed Dineen's striking out of "Hans" Wagner in the ninth equaled any college football game.

NEW YORK TIMES, OCTOBER 14, 1903

THE RED SOX

FANATIC

FOUR WORLD
CHAMPIONSHIPS IN SEVEN
YEARS

Beginning in 1912, the Red Sox assembled some stellar teams. The franchise added four World Championships to its collection, with triumphs in the Autumn Classic over a heavily favored Giants team in 1912, the Phillies in 1915, the Dodgers in 1916, and the Cubs in 1918.

1912

Nineteen-ten is a year to be remembered by Boston fans, as it was the year its great outfield combination, Duffy Lewis, Tris Speaker and Harry Hooper, first functioned together.

FRANK LIEB

Whenever a man has the goods he finds an opening, and so it came that the young Californian [Duffy Lewis] left the land of oranges to work in the City of Beans.

J. C. KOFOED

The Red Sox were renowned for the best outfield ever assembled to that time—and one of the finest ever.

TIMOTHY M. GAY

. . . **Speaker, Hooper and Lewis.** They're sure death on fly balls, and very few grounders ever get through them. Batting? This Speaker is a rare slugger, and Duffy Lewis hits close enough to .300 to make rival pitchers uncomfortable. Yes, I know Harry Hooper's batting average isn't anyways near as large as Cobb's, but he is one of the best run getters I ever saw.

BILL CARRIGAN, RED SOX PLAYER-MANAGER

Tris Speaker

[F]ew outfielders were capable of following Speaker's pattern. He played the shallowest center field ever seen before or since his time.

GORDON COBBLEDICK, *CLEVELAND PLAIN DEALER*

In a game during his rookie season, Joe DiMaggio played a centerfield so shallow that a fly ball that would normally be a routine out fell behind DiMaggio for a game-winning extra base hit. The losing pitcher, Yankee great Lefty Gomez, confronted DiMaggio in the clubhouse after the loss.

Why were you playing so shallow on the ball that got over your head, kid?

LEFTY GOMEZ

I'm going to make 'em forget Tris Speaker.

JOE DIMAGGIO

If you keep playing that shallow, you'll make 'em forget Lefty Gomez.

LEFTY GOMEZ TO JOE DIMAGGIO

Harry Hooper

Harry B. Hooper, right-fielder of the Boston Red Sox, and one of the original "Speed Boys" who will be the first man to toe the plate in the big fracas, is one of the very best men in the country to lead off a batting order.

PHILADELPHIA INQUIRER

Like Speaker, Hooper was to write many brilliant chapters in Red Sox history. If Tris was the game's foremost center fielder, many believe Hooper was the king of baseball's right field on the defense.

FRANK LIEB

Carrigan, Carrigan

Speaker, Lewis, Wood and Stahl

Bradley, Engle, Pape and Hall

Wagner, Gardner, Hooper, too.

Hit them! Hit them! Hit them! Hit

them!

Do, boys, do!

REFRAIN OF RED SOX FANS DURING THE 1912 WORLD SERIES,
SUNG TO THE TUNE OF "TAMMANY"

Domination of the Yankees

Before 1921 there was no great Red Sox–Yankees rivalry. Before then, the Yankees, or the Highlanders as they were called through 1912, contended for an American League pennant only two times. They finished just behind Boston in 1904 and three games behind Chicago's Hitless Wonders in 1906. In 1910 they finished second, but trailed the mighty Athletics by fourteen and a half games. The next year, their fortunes began to fall, and the New Yorkers spent four straight years in the second division. The Red Sox dominated the New York franchise thoroughly during this period, especially during their drive toward the first of four World Championships in seven years. From October 3, 1911 through July 1, 1912, the Red Sox went undefeated against the Yankees, beating New York in seventeen consecutive games.

Too much of this sort of thing is more than a-plenty. All season long the Yankees have submitted meekly to being trimmed by the Boston Red Sox and have never whimpered. But along came Boston yesterday, and not satisfied with a daily victory, imposed on good nature and grabbed two in one afternoon. That's no way to make friends.

NEW YORK TIMES, JUNE 23, 1912

Smoky Joe Wood

I've seen some pretty fair pitching, but I've never seen anything like Smoky Joe Wood in 1912.

HARRY HOOPER

Can I throw harder than Joe Wood? Listen mister, no man alive can throw any harder than Smoky Joe Wood.

WALTER JOHNSON

Pedro Martinez? Roger Clemens? Babe Ruth? Awesome Red Sox pitchers all, but none of them ever approached Joe Wood in 1912.

THE DIAMOND ANGLE

I threw so hard [in Game 1 of the 1912 World Series] I thought my arm would fly right off my body.

SMOKY JOE WOOD

[My arm] was in a cast for two or three weeks. I don't know whether I tried to pitch too soon after that, or whether maybe something happened to my shoulder at the same time. But whatever it was, I never pitched again without a terrific amount of pain in my right shoulder. Never again.

SMOKY JOE WOOD

The Rebirth of Smoky Joe

Smoky Joe Wood's 1912 season was the greatest ever by a Red Sox pitcher. Cy Young twice won more than thirty games for the new American League franchise. He posted a record of 33–10 with thirty-eight complete games, 384 2/3 innings pitched, and an ERA of 1.62 in 1901 and followed it with a mark of 32–11, forty-one complete games, 341 2/3 innings pitched, and an ERA of 2.15 in 1902. But, in 1912, Wood posted a record that surpassed even those awesome numbers. Wood went 34–5, posted an .872 winning percentage, and recorded thirty-five complete games, 344 innings pitched, and an ERA of 1.91. He won three games and lost one in the 1912 World Series.

Smoky Joe, as his moniker suggests, threw very hard, and the grind in 1912 took its toll. In his next three seasons, Wood posted characteristically high winning percentages, but his win totals were meager compared to 1912. In 1915, he recorded his highest figure for wins after 1912 with fifteen. But his fifteenth win that year would be the last of his career.

In 1918, Wood made a comeback as a position player. By now, he was an Indian. His primary position was the outfield, where he played beside the great former Red Sox star Tris Speaker. He also played a handful of games at second base and at first. His comeback was a success. He posted averages of .296 in 1918 and .297 in 1922, and .366 in a sixty-six-game stint in 1921. His value to the Cleveland club may be gauged by manager Speaker's decision to play Wood in the outfield for four games in the 1920 World Series.

1912 World Series

This was a nip-and-tuck series, with the favorite becoming the underdog and fighting back from a 3–2 deficit to bring matters all even again—only to blow the prize with a brace of errors that would have enraged a high school coach.

ROBERT SMITH

The advantage in the 1912 World Series shifted between the teams, ricocheting like a pinball through the last, extra inning of the final game. The Red Sox took Game 1 in New York, 2–1. Game 2 was called on account of darkness after eleven innings and ended in a 6–6 tie. The Giants evened the series with a 2–1 win at Fenway Park in Game 3. The Red Sox won Games 4 and 5, to take a three games to one lead, but the Giants surged back with a Game 6 victory at the Polo Grounds and an 11–5 drubbing of the Red Sox in Boston in Game 7. The series was notorious for fielding lapses. The Giants made seventeen errors in the eight games, the Red Sox fourteen. Giants shortstop Art Fletcher alone made three errors in Game 2. The series would be decided by some of the most inexplicable defensive incompetence ever at the major league level. The Red Sox made five of their fourteen errors in the first nine innings of Game 8. The Giants, however, would outdo the Red Sox and their own elevated standard of ineptitude to abdicate the World Series crown.

Write in the pages of world's series baseball history the name of Snodgrass. Write it large and black.

NEW YORK TIMES, OCTOBER 17, 1912

In the final game, the great Christy Mathewson and Red Sox rookie right-hander Hugh Bedient battled to a 1–1 tie after nine innings. The Giants took a 2–1 lead in the top of the tenth inning on a single off Smoky Joe Wood by first baseman Fred Merkle. Folly of historic dimensions would reverse the fortunes of the teams in the bottom of the inning. Pinch hitter Cliff Engle led off for the Red Sox and precipitated one of the most notorious errors in World Series play. *The New York Times* described the play with the elegiac tones of high tragedy:

Is Mathewson apprehensive as he walks to the box? He is not. All the confidence that was his when his blood of youth ran strong in his supple muscles is his now. He shows not a quiver, and he is right. All that Engle can do with the elusive drop served up is to hoist it high between centre and right fields. Snodgrass and Murray are both within reach of it, with time to spare. Snodgrass yells, "I've got it," and sets himself to take it with ease, as he has taken hundreds of this sort. And now the ball settles. It is full and fair in the pouch of the padded glove of Snodgrass. But he is too eager to toss it to Murray and it dribbles to the ground. Before Snodgrass can hurl the ball to second Engle is perching there.

NEW YORK TIMES, OCTOBER 17, 1912

Snodgrass had made a game-saving catch in Game 3. He also robbed Harry Hooper, the next hitter after Engle, of extra bases with a spectacular over-the-shoulder catch in deepest left-centerfield and prevented the tying run from scoring. Only the gaffe is famous. The error by Snodgrass would not be the last by the Giants on a routine play, however. After Snodgrass's circus catch of Hooper's drive, Mathewson's poise and concentration abandoned him. He walked second baseman Steve Yerkes to put the winning run on base and bring the great Tris Speaker to the plate. Speaker popped the ball up in foul territory. When first baseman Merkle and catcher Chief Meyers converged on the ball, Mathewson charged toward the pop, called Merkle off, and told catcher Chief Meyers to make the play instead. Some sources even suggest that Speaker called off Merkle. In any event, Merkle deferred to Meyers. The catcher could not reach the foul, however, and it fell harmlessly to the ground. Speaker taunted Mathewson.

Well, you just called for the wrong man. It's gonna cost you this ball game.

TRIS SPEAKER

Speaker singled to right on Mathewson's next pitch, scoring Engle, and sending Yerkes to third. Mathewson then walked the dangerous Duffy Lewis intentionally. Third baseman Larry Gardner followed with a long fly to Josh Devore in right field. Devore's throw to home was true, but too late to catch Yerkes with the game and series-winning run.

Mathewson was magnanimous to Snodgrass in defeat:

No use hopping on him, he feels three times as bad as any of us.

CHRISTY MATHEWSON

Despite defensive play by the Giants that would drive a little league coach to despair, the *New York Times* contended that the Giants had actually won the championship.

Too bad! Too bad! The world championship belongs in New York and Boston is perfectly aware of it.

NEW YORK TIMES, OCTOBER 17, 1912

1915

Two thirds of the legendary Red Sox outfield played well in 1912. Harry Hooper hit .290. Tris Speaker hit .300. The remaining third of that great trio, Duffy Lewis, had a dismal series, batting .156 and fielding .933. Duffy's day came in 1915, when he hit in the clutch, recorded a batting average of .444 and a slugging average of .667, led all players in RBIs, and played flawlessly in the field.

Duffy Lewis was the real hero of this Series. I have witnessed all of the contests for the game's highest honors in the last 30 years, and I want to say that the all-around work of the modest Californian never has been equaled in a big Series.

TOM MURNAME, *BOSTON GLOBE*

Eliminate Lewis' work in the World's Series and Moran's men [the Phillies] would have reversed the result of those games. His daredevil fielding chopped down Quaker rallies, while his big bat personally brought three victories.

J. C. KOFOED

1918

Boston clubs have never lost a World Series, and the championship deserves to remain here until the war is over.

HARRY FRAZEE

The final game was played before the smallest crowd yet, local fans having turned against the ball players for their "greed" and "commercialism" in wanting to take home almost as much from the series as the club officials did.

ROBERT SMITH

Commercialism reigned, indeed. The players may have been greedy, according to public assessments, but Frazee outdid them, making good his pledge to keep the championship in Boston until the war was over and not a day longer.

Humbling the Greatest

During their run of four World Championships, the Red Sox repeatedly beat the best pitchers of the day, some of the greatest pitchers the game has ever produced. In 1912, Christy Mathewson went winless in three appearances against Boston. He was the victim of inept defense, of course, but he succumbed to clutch hitting by the Red Sox, as well. In Game 8, Tris Speaker and pinch hitter Olaf Henriksen drove in key runs with solid hits off Mathewson and, with a lead in the tenth inning, Mathewson issued a walk that put the winning run on base and allowed Tris Speaker to come to bat with the tying run in scoring position. Only two of the six runs Mathewson yielded over those eleven innings in Game 2 were earned, but Big Six lost Game 5 by a 2–1 score on consecutive triples and an error. The result: an ERA of 1.57, but a record of 0–2 and 1. The great Grover Cleveland Alexander won thirty-one games in 1915 and shut down the Red Sox in Game 1. But that was to be the Phillies' only victory of the series. Dutch Leonard's left arm and Duffy Lewis's ninth-inning double overcame Alexander in Game 3. The Red Sox lost two games to Hall of Fame southpaw Rube Marquard in 1912, but beat him twice without a loss in 1916. In 1918, Boston victimized the Cubs' twenty-two-game winner Hippo Vaughn twice in three decisions.

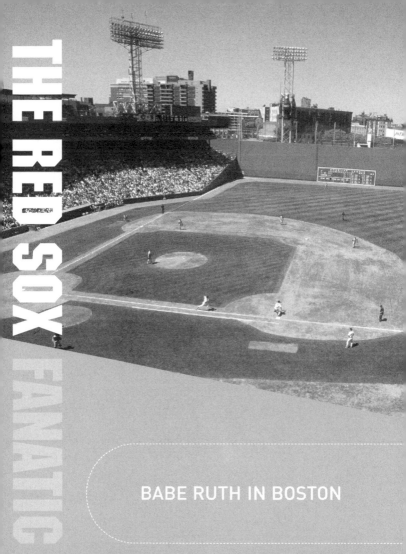

THE RED SOX FANATIC

BABE RUTH IN BOSTON

[The Babe] would sometimes cook up a two-pound steak, using a quart of chili sauce as flavoring, and then go to bed and sleep as peacefully as a child.

RED SMITH

I think my mother hated me.

BABE RUTH

If it wasn't for baseball I'd be either in the penitentiary or the cemetery.

BABE RUTH

Well, you know, Granny, Duke Ellington said the Battle of Waterloo was won on the playing fields of Elkton.

BABE RUTH, GETTING HIS DUKES AND HIS LOCATIONS CONFUSED. THE BABE MARRIED HIS FIRST WIFE IN ELKTON, MARYLAND. THE DUKE OF WELLINGTON ATTENDED ETON.

As soon as I got out there I felt a strange relationship with the pitcher's mound. It was as if I'd been born out there. Pitching just felt like the most natural thing in the world. Striking out batters was easy.

BABE RUTH

There is one thing better than hitting a home run. That one thing is pitching and winning a World Series game. That's the truth.

BABE RUTH

Certainly, Ruth's native [pitching] ability was prodigious. He might have become the greatest of all—but baseball history would have been inconceivably different.

LEONARD KOPPETT

Gee, it's lonesome in the outfield. It's hard to keep awake with nothing to do.

BABE RUTH

Ruth made a grave mistake when he gave up pitching. Working once a week he might have lasted a long time and become a great star.

TRIS SPEAKER

You run me out and I will come in there and bust you on the nose.

BABE RUTH, TO UMPIRE BRICK OWENS

Perfection in Relief

Babe Ruth's temper made possible one of the greatest pitching feats in baseball history. On June 23, 1917, Babe Ruth made good his threat to slug umpire Brick Owens if Owens threw Ruth out of the game. Ruth, the starting pitcher for the Red Sox against the Senators at Fenway Park, took issue with Owens's calls on Ray Morgan, the Washington leadoff hitter. Owens called four straight balls, and Ruth told the ump to open his eyes. Owens, notorious for a short fuse, threatened to run Ruth out of the game, if he didn't resume pitching. Ruth threatened to hit him if he did, and Owens immediately ejected him. The Babe then charged home plate. Ruth began swinging with both hands before Owens had removed his mask and hit Owens behind the ear. Red Sox manager Jack Barry and several policemen dragged Ruth off the field, and right-hander Ernie Shore came in to pitch.

Catcher Sam Agnew threw Morgan out on a steal attempt. With the help of a great play by shortstop Everett Scott and two by Duffy Lewis, one up his famous "cliff," Shore retired all of the remaining twenty-six Senators he faced. Whether or not the game qualifies as a perfect game, Shore was perfect.

He [Manager Jack Barry] asked me if I'd pitch until he could get someone else warmed up.

ERNIE SHORE

THE RED SOX

FANATIC

HARRY FRAZEE AND THE
DISMANTLING OF A DYNASTY

Someone asked me . . . if my club was for sale. What a ridiculous question. Of course, it is for sale. So is my hat and my overcoat, and my watch. Anyone who wants them can have them at a reasonable price. I will dispose of my holdings in the Red Sox at any time for my price.

HARRY FRAZEE

As luck would have it, Harry Frazee's New York City office on Broadway was only a block away from Col. Jack Ruppert's, the majority owner of the New York Yankees. This made it easy for Frazee to sell off piecemeal parts of the Red Sox to keep his head above water.

WILLIAM A. COOKE

The best thing about Boston is the train ride back to New York.

HARRY FRAZEE

Babe Ruth of the Boston Red Sox, baseball's super-slugger, was purchased by the Yankees yesterday for the largest cash sum ever paid for a player. The New York club paid Harry Frazee of Boston $125,000 for the sensational batsman who last season caused such a furor in the national game by batting out 29 home runs, a new record in long-distance clouting. . . . The acquisition of Ruth strengthens the Yankee club in its weakest department. . . . For several seasons the Yankees have been experimenting with outfielders, but never have been able to land a consistent hitter. The short right field wall at the Polo Grounds should prove an easy target for Ruth next season, and, playing 77 games at home, it would not be surprising if Ruth surpassed his home-run record of 29 circuit clouts next Summer.

NEW YORK TIMES, JANUARY 6, 1920

When they sold Ruth, the very next day signs appeared in the Boston Common and in front of the Boston Public Library that said, "For Sale." Because that's how struck people were with the fact that Ruth was sold. You might have sold the Boston Common or the Boston Public Library.

GLENN STUART

The Yankee dynasty of the twenties was three-quarters the Red Sox of a few years before. All [Red Sox owner Harry] Frazee wanted was the money. He was short of cash and he sold the whole damn team down the river to keep his dirty nose above water. What a way to end a wonderful ball club!

HARRY HOOPER

To my mind, no individual player in so uncertain a profession as baseball is worth any such sum of money. Ruth made 29 home runs last year, but no one knows what he will do next year.

HARRY FRAZEE

[Harry Frazee] ruined one of America's great ball clubs by systematically selling star after star to the rich owners of the Yankees, Col. Jake Ruppert and Col. T.L. Husten.

BOSTON GLOBE

Harry Frazee

Harry Frazee, a Broadway producer whose success was inconsistent and intermittent, maintained residences in both Boston and New York. A lover of baseball, he apparently preferred rubbing shoulders with entertainers to maintaining a stable of winning athletes. Through the mid-1920s, Frazee was notorious for backing losers on Broadway. He was the kind of investor whose losses in one endeavor drag other, profitable enterprises into ruin. Frazee regarded the Red Sox as just another investment. He was blunt in his acknowledgment that he owed nothing to the millions of fans who made the team a lucrative business. More important, he was clever enough to profit enormously from his own mismanagement.

During the successful run of a production in 1917, Frazee bought the Red Sox for $400,000. The next year the team would win the World Series for the fourth time in seven years. But, beginning in 1919, Frazee's financial woes induced him to trade star players, including disgruntled pitcher Carl Mays and the twenty-four-year-old Babe Ruth, to the Yankees, to borrow $300,000 from New York owner Jacob Ruppert, and give Ruppert a mortgage on Fenway Park. Under this blatant conflict of interest, the Red Sox became the vassal of the New York franchise, and a team that had never won a pennant began building a decades-long dynasty from the Red Sox roster. By the time *No No Nanette* and its hit song "Tea for Two" first earned him lasting success on Broadway in 1925, Frazee had run the Red Sox into the cellar. In 1923, Frazee sold the franchise for $1.5 million, a 300-percent profit. Beats working for a living.

Get up—get up, it's here, it's here.
Your Christmas present is here.

AD HOYT, INFORMING HIS SON, WAITE HOYT OF HIS TRADE FROM
THE RED SOX TO THE YANKEES ON DECEMBER 15, 1920

There had been hell to pay in 1922 when the Red Sox traded [third baseman Joe] Dugan to New York. With Home Run Baker slowing down—he had been the regular third baseman since 1916—the Yankees had gone to Boston for help on July 23, raising furious charges that they were trying to "buy a pennant." The deal brought about a rule setting June 1 as the deadline for trades.

RED SMITH

My sole object, since coming to Boston, has been to give the public a winning team. And personally, I think this latest deal will take its place along with the rest, for I believe that the sale of Ruth will ultimately strengthen the team.

HARRY FRAZEE

Prior to 1921 the New York Yankees had never won an American League pennant and had done no better than finishing second in 1904, 1906, and 1910. Now thanks to the generosity of Harry Frazee, the New York Yankees would win six American League pennants in the next eight years.

WAITE HOYT

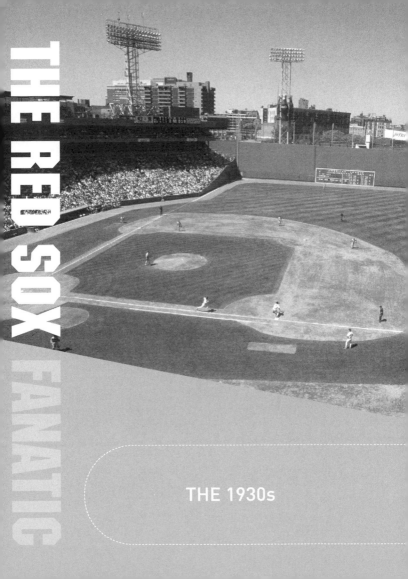

THE RED SOX FANATIC

THE 1930s

[Lefty Grove's] fastball was so fast that, by the time you'd made up your mind whether it would be a strike or not, it just wasn't there anymore.

CHARLIE GEHRINGER

Lefty Grove could throw a pork chop past a wolf.

SPORTSWRITER'S ASSESSMENT

Oh my yes, Joe is the best there is in the clutch. With a man on third and one out, I'd rather have Cronin hitting for me than anybody I've ever seen.

CONNIE MACK

The First Red Sox Batting Champion

In June 1932, the Red Sox traded Earl Webb, one of the league's leading sluggers, to the Tigers for two players. One was Dale Alexander, a sweet-swinging first baseman. The press treated Webb as the marquee player, but Alexander proved to be the prize. Webb fell off from a .333 batting average in 1931 to marks of .285 in 1932 and .288 in 1933. By 1934, Webb was out of baseball. Alexander came to Boston with a .250 average, but hit .372 in his 101 games for Boston. Although Jimmy Foxx had three hits in his final game of the season with the Athletics, Alexander's two hits in the Red Sox season finale gave him an average of .367 for the year, three points higher than the mark set by the Beast. Foxx led the league in several offensive categories including, by a large margin, home runs with 58 and RBIs with 169. The Red Sox first baseman thus cost Foxx the Triple Crown.

Alexander later suffered a debilitating injury at the hands of the Red Sox trainer. Doc Woods, a chiropractor, treated Alexander for a leg injury in the Boston clubhouse by focusing a heat lamp on the damaged limb. While Alexander contentedly read a book, Woods proceeded to the Red Sox bench and watched the game in progress. Doc became absorbed by a Red Sox rally, and by the time he remembered his patient, Alexander's leg had been sufficiently scalded to sideline him for weeks.

Wes [Ferrell] had a terrible temper. . . . One time he got taken out of a ballgame. He was so gol-dern mad. He wanted to throw his glove into the dugout just before he went down the steps, but he missed the dugout and threw it into the stands.

FABIAN GAFFKE

Ruppert bought some pennants, when he was able to reach into the Red Sox for players. But, it doesn't seem to work for us when we buy Mack's old champions. So we've got to try something else and raise our own.

TOM YAWKEY

A New Meaning to Heads-up Play

On September 7, 1935, the Red Sox were trailing the Indians 5–1 in Fenway Park in the ninth inning of the first game of a doubleheader. The Red Sox mounted a rally. They scored two runs and put two runners on with none out. Hall of Fame shortstop Joe Cronin lined a pitch down the third base line for an apparent hit, possibly one for extra bases that could have tied the game. The good news is that it eluded the glove of the Cleveland third baseman. But bad news prevailed in two senses. First the third baseman was Odell "Bad News" Hale. On that day he lived up to his name—in spades. The ball struck Hale in the head and ricocheted to shortstop Bill Knickerbocker. Knickerbocker caught the ball in the air for out number one and threw to second baseman Terry Hughes for out number two. Hughes then fired on to first baseman Hal Trosky, who retired Red Sox outfielder Mel Almada for a game-ending triple play.

THE RED SOX FANATIC

A DRUBBING FOR THE AGES

Fenway Park is the Fairy Godmother of offensive records: the most doubles in a season, the most doubles in a career, the most runs in an inning, the most runs scored by one team in one game.

On June 8, 1950, the Red Sox unleashed a nuclear assault on the forlorn St. Louis Browns. Boston sent sixty-eight men to the plate, knocked out twenty-eight hits, and compiled sixty total bases. The Sox had two two-run innings, two five-run innings, one seven-run inning, and one eight-run inning. That adds up to twenty-nine runs, a modern major league record. Eleven Red Sox walked. Catcher Matt Batts doubled once. Johnny Pesky doubled twice. Junior Stephens doubled and tripled. Al Zarilla doubled four times. Ted Williams and Walt Dropo hit two home runs each. Bobby Doerr hit three. Mercy!

The next day, the Associated Press published a photograph of Ted Williams after it was over, one of the greatest students of baseball the sport ever produced standing in leftfield, hands on hips, gazing at the huge score on the huge scoreboard, his imagination transfixed and his credulity taxed.

THE RED SOX

FANATIC

TED WILLIAMS, THE HITTER

Confidence oozed out of him. He took something away from you even before you threw a pitch.

GENE CONLEY

His swing was long, much longer than Ruth's . . . and beautiful the way Sam Snead's swing is beautiful, all body parts working together and the ball just an incident in the course of the arc.

JOHN UPDIKE

Get a good ball to hit.

ROGERS HORNSBY, TO THE YOUNG TED WILLIAMS

I told those guys [the Red Sox outfield of Joe Vosmik, Doc Cramer, and Ben Chapman] that I'd make more money in one year than all three of them combined.

TED WILLIAMS, UPON BEING DEMOTED TO THE MINORS, 1938

[Ted Williams] studied hitting the way a broker studies the stock market, and could spot at a glance mistakes that others couldn't see in a week.

CARL YASTRZEMSKI

A lot of people have as good eyesight as I have (20-15) and probably better, and still they're always ready to say, "Eyesight's the reason he does it and natural ability." . . . They never talk about the practice. Practice! Practice! Practice! Dammit, you gotta practice.

TED WILLIAMS

[H]e wakes up at seven o'clock every morning. He stands in front of a mirror with a hairbrush, holding it like a bat, and he scowls in the mirror, like he's facing a pitcher, and he growls. "Come on, you big so and so. Put it over the plate and I'll drive it down your throat."

CHARLIE WAGNER, RED SOX PITCHER AND ROOMMATE OF THE ROOKIE TED WILLIAMS

No one can ever see the ball hit the bat, because it's physically impossible to focus your eyes that way. However, when I hit the ball exceptionally hard, I could smell the leather start to burn as it hit the wooden bat.

TED WILLIAMS

Hitting is 50 percent above the shoulders.

TED WILLIAMS

Did they tell me how to pitch to Williams? Sure they did. It was great advice, very encouraging. They said he had no weakness, won't swing at a bad ball, has the best eyes in the business, and can kill you with one swing. He won't hit anything bad, but don't give him anything good.

BOBBY SHANTZ

When you start going for a pitch an inch off, the next time that pitcher will throw it two inches off, then three, and before you know it you're hitting .250.

TED WILLIAMS

If I couldn't hit .400 all the way I didn't deserve it.

TED WILLIAMS, ON HIS REFUSAL TO SKIP THE LAST DOUBLE HEADER WITH A .39955 AVERAGE

When Williams went to bat in the second game . . . shortstop Boudreau concentrated six men in right field. The Cleveland manager played on the grass midway between first and second. Jimmy Wasdell, the first sacker, posted himself on the grass near the foul line. The third baseman was on the grass on the right side of second base and the right and center fielders patrolled as deep as possible in that sector.

NEW YORK TIMES, JULY 15, 1946, ON THE FIRST SHIFT AGAINST TED WILLIAMS

I hated to go to left field because I felt it was a sign of weakness.

TED WILLIAMS, ON THE SHIFT

Ted Williams is not a team man, he is utterly lacking in anything that even bears remote resemblance to team spirit.

DAVE EGAN, *BOSTON GLOBE*

[O]ne reason for the shift was that the defense was more afraid of a homer than a single, and by taking the single, Williams would be playing the defense's game. . . . A homer could win a game better than a single—and if the hitter were as good as Williams was, it was worth the try.

LEONARD KOPPETT

Ted was the greatest hitter of our era.

STAN MUSIAL

A Gracious Tribute

The White Sox were one of the first teams to celebrate their home runs by shooting off fireworks. When Ted Williams came to Chicago chasing 500 home runs during the 1960 season, the White Sox planned to shoot off fireworks if The Kid hit his five hundredth blast in their park. This was the only time that the White Sox offered the tribute to a visiting player. Williams didn't go long in Chicago, though. He hit dinger number 500 in Cleveland's Municipal Stadium.

The race for the distinction of being the greatest hitter of all time as measured by formal analysis is between Ruth and Williams, and it is so close that any revision of the method, however small, is likely to reverse the outcome.

BILL JAMES

I remember one day in September when I was on second base and I looked at home, and I said, "Boy, that's a long ways." And I knew it was time to go.

TED WILLIAMS

One and one to Williams. Everybody quiet now here at Fenway Park after they gave him a standing ovation of two minutes, knowing that this is probably his last time at bat. One out, nobody on, last of the eighth inning. Jack Fisher into his windup. Here's the pitch. Williams swings. And there's a long drive to deep right. That ball is going. It is gone.

CURT GOWDY

THE RED SOX FANATIC

TED WILLIAMS, THE FANS,
AND THE PRESS

Greatness necessarily attracts debunkers, but in Williams' case the hostility has been systematic and unappeasable.

JOHN UPDIKE

Ted Williams's relations with the press, and with some fans, were notoriously antagonistic. His undisguised hatred of the press began with vitriolic criticism he suffered during his second year with the Red Sox. Williams joined the Red Sox in 1939 as an ingenuous twenty-year-old 3,000 miles from home. He was brash, outspoken, and exceedingly candid about his abilities. Even if he did not say that Jimmy Foxx would be amazed when he witnessed Williams's prowess at the plate, a statement frequently attributed to him but which Williams denies having made, his manner when he joined the Red Sox alienated his teammates.

Teddy is a spoiled boy. How long it will take him to grow up remains to be seen. But he'll have to grow up the hard way now.

JIMMY FOXX

The process was indeed painful and prolonged. The press saw to it. Williams said that he could never forget or overlook an article that attacked him. He had an equally great intolerance of disdain by the fans. There were incidents of obscene gestures and spitting toward the stands. Although Williams acknowledged that a tiny vocal minority of fans booed him, he refused to tip his cap, the customary response to fans' applause, beginning with his earliest years in Boston. The ovation for the home run in his last at bat in 1960 and a chant for an appearance from the dugout continued for minutes without an acknowledgment by the great hitter.

When Ted first came up in 1939, he played right field. After he'd hit a home run, he'd go out there and he'd take his cap off and hold it up, and fans would clap, and they just loved it.

BOBBY DOERR

Playing left field [in Fenway Park] is also unique, and there are fans who can lean right over and give you their venom at close range.

JACKIE JENSEN

In Boston, a man does not qualify as a baseball writer until he has psychoanalyzed Williams. Some of the more analytical scribes dissect him once a week, and a couple are suspected of taking him apart twice a day, partly for the edification of their readers, but largely for their own amusement.

HAROLD KAESE, *BOSTON GLOBE*

I was never able to be dispassionate, to ignore the things people said or wrote or implied. It just wasn't in me. In my heart I don't believe I am any more sensitive to criticism than a lot of athletes, but I am certainly in the upper bracket of sensitivity, maybe the top 3 per cent. In a crowd of cheers I could always pick out the solitary boo.

TED WILLIAMS

Oh, so you're a baseball writer. I never met you before, but you're no good. No good till you prove otherwise.

TED WILLIAMS

[W]illiams had studied The Wall the way Einstein studied relativity. He seldom had to hurry much to field any carom—so he was charged with jaking it, lollygagging around and dreaming while awaiting his next turn at bat.

GEORGE V. HIGGINS

You've sat sullen and aloof in locker rooms and hotels. Often you've looked lazy and careless on fly balls. Occasionally you've snarled things back at the bleacherites. You've taken the attitude, sometimes, that you're bigger than the game.

DUKE LAKE, *BOSTON AMERICAN*

Oh, he plays to win all right, and generally gives his best—or what he considers his best—but there is something lacking. The dimensions of the performance are heroic, but the effect isn't moving or genuine. It is like watching a superb Hollywood duelist in action. Wonderful. But you wouldn't want to bet on him to get you out of a jam.

JOE WILLIAMS, *SPORT* MAGAZINE

Anybody who saw him in the holiday double-header would say the Boston fans are justified in anything up to throwing him into the Charles River . . . his one long hit of the day was well belted, but he gave up and settled for a double.

JACK ORR, *NEW YORK COMPASS*

The inventor of the automatic choke.

DAVE EGAN

He is utterly lacking in anything that bears even a remote resemblance to team spirit or team pride. First and last and at all times in between he is for Ted Williams and Ted Williams alone.

DAVE EGAN

I want you to make it very clear that all the credit goes to Hughson. He pitched a helluva game. My home run didn't mean a thing when I hit it.

TED WILLIAMS, ON THE RED SOX CLINCHING THE 1946 PENNANT, 1–0

In the 10 most important games of his life, the great man batted .205 and knocked in one run.

DAVE EGAN

I never did make an excuse for my poor performance. For sure, I was taking antibiotics, and I also had been hit on the elbow, and I, gee, did nothing. I couldn't even think straight on the damn thing. I don't know what the hell happened.

TED WILLIAMS, ON HIS DISMAL 1946 WORLD SERIES

[Jackie] Jensen has won more than a dozen games with his bat alone, while whole posses of citizens could scour the records without ever finding a solitary game which the bat of Ted Williams has won.

DAVE EGAN

Pitcher Jack Kramer, slugger Ted Williams, and seven alert Boston Red Sox colleagues this afternoon knocked the New York Yankees out of all chance to win the American League pennant. . . . Both teams made the same number of hits—five. But the first Boston hit, Williams' No. 25 homer . . . won the ball game. . . . [A] double by Williams, was the essential swat in the production of two comforting runs in the third inning.

EDWARD BURNS, *CHICAGO DAILY TRIBUNE,* OCTOBER 2, 1948

For the press to say that we would have won without Williams was nonsense. What a statement to make . . . the greatest hitter that ever lived.

WALT DROPO

Williams is a peculiar cuss, so tangled in his inner man that even a psychologist or psychiatrist would have trouble unraveling him. He is more hated than liked by those who know him best.

ARTHUR DALEY, *NEW YORK TIMES*

To get a real line on Williams you have to see his face in the clubhouse after a game which the Red Sox have won and in which he's gone hitless. That tells the story.

JACK ORR, *NEW YORK COMPASS*

I went into my little compartment on the train, and I didn't come out until about ten thirty. When I got in there and closed the door I just broke down and started crying, and I looked up and there was a whole crowd of people watching me through the window.

TED WILLIAMS, UPON LOSING THE 1946 WORLD SERIES

Williams is the prize heel ever to wear a Boston uniform.

DAVE EGAN

Few of his fans thought any more highly of Ted when it became known last winter that the great man went fishing in Florida while his wife journeyed to Boston to await the birth of their first child.

ED FITZGERALD

Williams acknowledged that he was in Florida when his daughter was born, but notes that she was born prematurely.

Well, what do you expect from a guy who
won't even go to see his mother in the off
season.

HAROLD KAESE

Ted Williams had served as a Marine pilot during World War II, although he did not see action. In 1952, Williams was summoned to combat duty in Korea. On April 30, the Red Sox held a day for Williams that was attended by 25,000 fans, the mayor, and the governor. A Boston newspaper prepared a memory book and gathered the signatures of 400,000 fans from all over the country for presentation during the ceremony. Williams flew numerous combat missions in Korea and was nearly incinerated in a plane that was hit by enemy fire and burst into flames shortly after landing. Dave Egan, a columnist for the *Globe* and the *Record* who called himself the Colonel, dissented from the outpouring of warmth in anticipation of Williams's departure for Korea.

If he [Dave Egan] writes nine bad columns and then one good one, I don't see why I'm supposed to forget the nine bad ones.

TED WILLIAMS

If somebody came in through that green door over there and said Dave Egan just dropped dead, I'd look at that sonofabitch and I'd say, Good!

TED WILLIAMS

Heck, he's just a great big kid
with an inferiority complex.

GRANTLAND RICE

Open War

Two incidents in 1956 demonstrated Ted Williams' hostility toward the press and fans who ridiculed him. In July, he hit his 400th home run. When he passed the press box during his home run trot, he spat in the direction of those he called the knights of the keyboard. In August fans booed him after he dropped a fly ball under rainy conditions. When fans cheered a running catch later in the same game, Teddy Ballgame spat toward the stands. One outburst cost him a $5,000 fine.

I know I'm not right spitting, but gee, it's the only thing I can think of doing. I don't want to smile at them. I don't want to wave my hat at them. I don't want to give them a fist job. All I can do is let a big heave, take in a lot of air and go phooey!

TED WILLIAMS

As it is, considering Williams' tax bracket,

chances are the federal government will pay about $3,500 of the fine, though it may cause some commotion around the Internal Revenue Bureau when a return comes in with a $5,000 deduction for spit.

RED SMITH, *NEW YORK TIMES*

There was great applause but no tip of the cap by Williams as he crossed the plate. At this late date in his career, Williams wasn't starting anything new. All his baseball life, caps had been for wearing, not tipping.

SHIRLEY POVICH

If he would just tip his cap once in a while, they would elect him mayor.

JACKIE JENSEN

Ultimately, Teddy Ballgame relented. In 1991, at Fenway Park, during the celebration of the 50th anniversary of his batting .406, Williams pulled a cap he had borrowed from Red Sox reliever Jeff Reardon out of his pocket and waved it to an adoring crowd.

If I were asked where I would like to have played, I would have to say Boston. . . . the greatest fans in America.

TED WILLIAMS

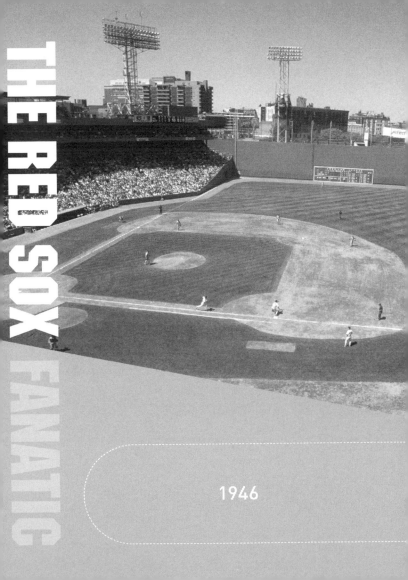

THE RED SOX

FANATIC

1946

With the end of World War II, hundreds of major league players returned to the game in 1946. Future hall of famer Bobby Doerr returned to the Red Sox from a year's absence. Ted Williams, Johnny Pesky, and Dom DiMaggio played in Fenway Park for the first time since 1942. Ted Williams won the Most Valuable Player award with a batting average of .342, 38 home runs, 123 runs batted in, and a league-high 142 runs scored. Veteran first baseman Rudy York drove in 119 runs. With catcher Charley Wagner completing a solid defense up the middle, Boo Ferris winning twenty-five games, Tex Hughson winning twenty, and Mickey Harris winning seventeen, the Red Sox rebounded from a seventh-place finish in 1945 to a 104-win season and the American League pennant by a twelve-game margin. Tom Yawkey, the legendary Red Sox owner, had bought the team in 1933, when it finished thirty-three games out of first place. It had taken thirteen years, but Yawkey had his first pennant.

We had to turn away over twenty-five thousand on a dozen occasions. On several Sundays, and when Feller pitched his first two games against us, we had to stop people as far away as a Kenmore Square, if they didn't have tickets.

ED DOHERTY, RED SOX PUBLICITY DIRECTOR

Bobby Doerr

[Bobby Doerr is] hardly ever spectacular on a play. He's just one of the guys who have hauled up the Red Sox from the second division to the top of the top of the American League.

RED SMITH

Bobby Doerr cannot recall being hammered by the Boston media or being insulted by the fans. Reasonable enough, because he was perceived as a workman, who always gave his very best. But those who won't, or don't, get ridiculed pitilessly.

GEORGE V. HIGGINS

I was never officially designated as captain but Teddy said things like, "Captain Bobby Doerr" and it stuck.

BOBBY DOERR

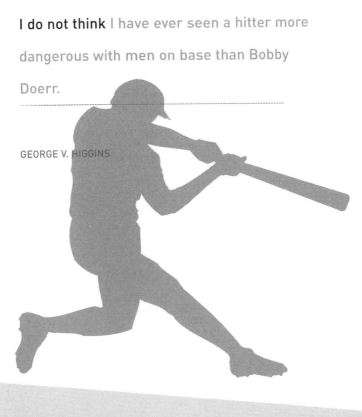

I do not think I have ever seen a hitter more dangerous with men on base than Bobby Doerr.

GEORGE V. HIGGINS

Johnny Pesky

So the Paveskovich solution was
Pesky, a name that was also descrip-
tive of his play on a baseball diamond.
He was indeed a pesky little fellow who
came up with balls around the infield
he had no right getting at, as well as
making a general nuisance of himself
as a hitter.

WARREN N. WILBERT

So this is the guy who's hittin' .340? How does he get his hits?

LUKE APPLING

See those dribbles and loopers? Those are his hits. All I know is, almost every time I look up, he's out there dancing around on first.

TED WILLIAMS

Hitting the Ground and the Ball Running

Johnny Pesky was not only one of the best defensive shortstops in the American League, he was also one of its best hitters. Pesky was the first player in major league history to collect 200 hits in each of his first three big league seasons. As a rookie in 1942, Pesky got 205 hits. After two seasons away from the game because of World War II, he returned to baseball and set marks of 208 hits in 1946 and 207 in 1947. Johnny led the league in hits in all three seasons.

Dom DiMaggio

With those glasses we better get him in the outfield.

CHARLIE GRAHAM, OWNER OF THE PACIFIC COAST LEAGUE SAN FRANCISCO SEALS

Dom could do everything. He could run like hell. He could throw. He was very smart. He played the hitters. And he got on base all the time.

ROY MUMPTON

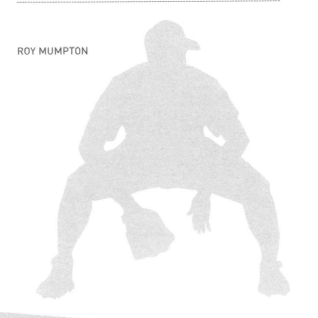

[O]ur oldest brother, Tom . . . [is] probably a bit shorter than I am but he could hit a ball farther than either Joe or Vince. Out in San Francisco they still point reverently to distant spots in the sandlot outfields and say, "That's where Tom DiMaggio hit one." They'd make it sound as though he were Babe Ruth. He could run like a deer and could field and throw better than any of us.

DOM DIMAGGIO

I was reading today, Joe about your brother Tom. How far could he hit a ball anyway?

CHARLIE KELLER

He could hit one over that bullpen out there. That's how good a
hitter he was.

JOE DIMAGGIO

Dom and Joe generated an intense rivalry between Red Sox and Yankee fans about which brother was the better outfielder. In Boston, the fans even sang a chant to the tune of "Maryland, my Maryland."

He's better than his brother Joe—Dominic DiMaggio.

BOSTON FANS' REFRAIN

Try it yourself, out loud. Not bad, eh?

ARTHUR DALEY, *NEW YORK TIMES*

As an outfielder he was just as good, or better, than his brother Joe, and they talk about Willie Mays and Hank Aaron, but I'll take Dom DiMaggio.

MATT BATTS

If his name were Smith or McGillicuddy, he'd already have been accepted as the superlative ball player he is. But Joe has raised the DiMaggio name to so high a plane that he alone can reach it.

ARTHUR DALEY

Boo and Tex

David "Boo" Ferris may have been the most talented pitcher the Red Sox developed between World War II and Roger Clemens. He was twenty-four when he won those twenty-five games in 1946, but he would appear in only seventy more games after that championship season, and only five after 1948. The science of orthopedics was primitive then compared to today. The radical career-saving technique for pitchers' arms known as Tommy John surgery was developed in the 1970s. If a pitcher had arm trouble in the 1940s, little could be done to relieve it, more often than not. Under Bill James's theory, too many innings, especially too many innings when tired, will be the ruin of a pitcher. A twenty-five-win season, by itself, can take a toll on a pitcher's arm. After a nine-year lackluster career, Steve Stone won twenty-five games for the Orioles in 1980. He said, "I knew it would ruin my arm, but one year of twenty-five wins is worth ten of 15–15." He was right. He managed only fifteen appearances in 1981 and was out of baseball the following year.

Tex Hughson won twenty games for the 1946 American League champions and then developed arm trouble. Hughson was a mainstay of the Red Sox rotation in the 1940s, winning eighteen games in 1944 and twenty-two in 1942, and leading the league in winning percentage in 1944. After 1946, however, he would record only nineteen career wins.

The early demise of Ferris and Hughson was, of course, disastrous for the Red Sox. A string of excruciating losses in seven-game World Series and in playoffs had begun in 1946. The bad luck continued in several close pennant races, beginning with the 1948 and 1949 seasons, and extended into the next century. A healthy Boo Ferris, or the availability of Tex Hughson or other Red Sox starters whose effectiveness had declined, would almost certainly have made the difference in the last two races of the 1940s. A meaningful contribution from any one of those pitchers would have brought the powerhouse 1946 team at least two more pennants, and banished the specter that would haunt the franchise until 2004.

Ferris acquired his nickname from his inability to pronounce the word brother as a youngster. "Boo" was the best he could manage. Hughson was called Tex because he was from Kyle, Texas, and because his given name was Cecil.

Slaughter's Mad Dash

The 1946 World Series was decided by Enos Slaughter's derring-do on the base paths. Slaughter made his "Mad Dash" with two out in the bottom of the eighth inning with the score tied in Game 7. Dom DiMaggio had been injured running the bases in the top of the inning and was replaced by Leon Culberson. Culberson was a good outfielder, but DiMaggio was one of the best. Slaughter was keenly aware that DiMaggio's powerful throwing arm was now out of the game.

On first with a single, Slaughter ran on a two-strike pitch to Harry "The Hat" Walker. Walker hit the ball over Johnny Pesky's head into leftfield. Slaughter continued around third and scored, when Pesky delayed throwing home.

Walker's hit was ruled a double by the official scorer, but many writers dispute the ruling. Walker's hit has been described as a "double, little more than a long single," (Frank Lieb) a "line drive over Johnny Pesky's head," (The

Sports Encyclopedia Baseball), and a "bloop . . . into centerfield that fell in front of Leon Culberson." (The Baseball Hall of Fame 50th Anniversary Book). If it were a genuine double, Slaughter's feat would be unremarkable. Many runners score from first on a double, especially with two outs. Slaughter's race to the plate is famous as the "Mad Dash," base running of historic audacity. Walker's hit must have looked like a single on the field. The fielders would not anticipate that a runner on first would attempt to score on a single.

Some sources blame outfielder Leon Culberson for bobbling the ball or for a feckless, casual throw to the infield. Slaughter considered Culberson not to be a "strong thrower," a key factor in his decision to head for home on what he described as Walker's "little floater" into the outfield. Tom Wicker and others note that Pesky was looking to throw to second, to prevent Walker from advancing. Pesky had veteran third baseman Mike Higgins on his right and Hall of Famer Bobby Doerr on his left, but neither succeeded in exhorting him to throw home.

Slaughter continued around third, and the relay throw from Pesky was just too late to prevent the go-ahead run. Pesky has been criticized for hesitating before throwing home.

Pesky was not a rookie. He had played 147 games in 1942, before losing three years to military service. He had played a full season in 1946. He was an excellent short-stop. His split-second hesitation would be consistent with a single rather than a double. At the very least, since Pesky took the throw with his back to the plate, he needed to be warned by his mates in the infield that Slaughter was headed for home.

Pesky had to go out and take the outfielder's throw and he couldn't see me, what with his back to the plate. It was up to his teammates to yell to him, but nobody did. You couldn't blame Pesky. By the time he turned around and got ready to throw, I was just a step or two away from the plate.

ENOS SLAUGHTER

Pesky was a very smart ballplayer. Doerr hollered at him, and he couldn't understand Doerr. He held the ball. He would have had a play on Slaughter at third base if he had thrown it. . . . Doerr was hollering "third" and Pesky couldn't understand him because the crowd was going crazy. And Slaughter scored.

ROY MUMPTON

I would have needed a rifle to nail Slaughter.

JOHNNY PESKY

I got blamed for something I didn't think was my fault. It always comes up. About three weeks ago I was in the market, and a guy climbed all over me. "You're a bum." He was an older guy. I said, "You weren't even there." He said he was. I said, "Where did this play occur?" He said, "In Boston." And it had occurred in St. Louis.

JOHNNY PESKY

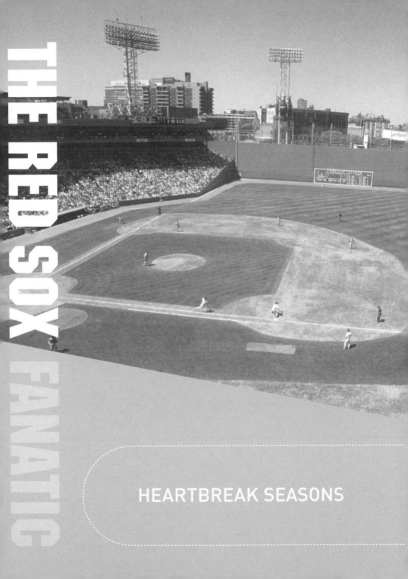

THE RED SOX

FANATIC

HEARTBREAK SEASONS

1948

[T]he daffiest pennant jamboree
the American League has ever
been able to stage . . .

IRVING VAUGHN

[I]t's just too jumbled a state for any firm opinion to be formed. The Bosox lead the Yanks by a game and the Indians by a game and a half. . . . But picking a winner is like trying to pick a winning number in a roulette game.

ARTHUR DALEY, *NEW YORK TIMES*, SEPTEMBER 3, 1948

American League Standings on October 1, 1948

	W.	L.	P. C.
Cleveland	95	57	.625
New York	94	58	.618
Boston	94	58	.618

There are seven possible outcomes. The Indians, Yankees or Red Sox could win outright, there could be a tie between any two of them and they could finish in a three-way deadlock.

NEW YORK TIMES, OCTOBER 2

All Boston hung on to loudspeakers throughout the afternoon to hear the details from Cleveland. For another Indian victory would assure them a tie. . . . . . [Boston] Manager Joe McCarthy spent the day in his hotel room, listening to radio reports.

LOS ANGELES TIMES, OCTOBER 1

The Cleveland Indians hit the road again today and finally reached a point just around the corner from the American League pennant goal. They massacred the Tigers, 8 to 0, in the penultimate battle of the blistery campaign, thus ensuring a tie with the Red Sox, who with their triumph over the Yankees, remained one lap behind Lou Boudreau's pace-setters.

IRVING VAUGHN, *CHICAGO DAILY TRIBUNE*, OCTOBER 3

Pitcher Jack Kramer, slugger Ted Williams, and seven alert Boston Red Sox colleagues this afternoon knocked the New York Yankees out of all chance to win the American League pennant. . . . As for the retiring world champions—the best they can do is beat the Red Sox here tomorrow for a second place tie.

EDWARD BURNS, *CHICAGO DAILY TRIBUNE*, OCTOBER 3

He was dumbfounded. He was shagging flies in the outfield during batting practice when McCarthy sent a clubhouse man for him. When Joe told them, Denny was white as a ghost.

MEL PARNELL, ON DENNY GALEHOUSE LEARNING THAT HE WOULD START THE PLAYOFF GAME AGAINST CLEVELAND

[Bill Veeck's] team had blown a two-game lead in the last three games of the season. His pitching staff was used up, his club's morale was presumably shattered, and the Red Sox were on the crest of a wave, freshly reclaimed from the mortuary . . . [Gene Bearden] has a metal plate in his head and a metal hinge in his knee. But he held the Red Sox to five hits. . . . [and] they gave Boston back to the Indians.

RED SMITH

1949

Boston finished second both years
[1948 and 1949], one game out of first
place. These Red Sox were no longer
a laughable lot. Instead, they were
muscle-flexing silver medalists.

DAN SHAUGHNESSY

[T]he locker room, it was silent. Like we were all dead. . . . Me, I couldn't talk. I could not speak at all. I felt as if someone had died.

TED WILLIAMS

It's hard winning a pennant, but it's harder losing one.

CHUCK TANNER

What I liked about this game, the rogues win it.

GARRY SCHUMACHER

Isn't it **wonderful,** Dominic, now we can go on vacation right away.

EMILY DIMAGGIO, TO HER HUSBAND, DOMINIC

1978

You cannot come in here and challenge our lineup. It's like punching a tar baby. The harder you hit it the more trouble you're in.

BILL LEE

Today is the biggest game of my life.

CARL YASTRZEMSKI, ON THE PLAYOFF GAME WITH THE YANKEES

Spaced Out

Bill Lee was eccentric and outspoken. His outspokenness cost him and the Red Sox dearly in 1978. Educated at the University of Southern California, he was a staunch traditionalist in baseball matters, vocal in his opposition to artificial turf, the designated hitter rule and double-knit uniforms. But in other ways, he was edgy, to say the least. Lee practiced yoga and claimed that marijuana immunized him from the effects of bus fumes that filled the air when he jogged through Boston to Fenway Park. He attracted a circle of eccentric players in the Boston clubhouse, a group that called itself the Royal Order of the Buffalo Heads. In 1988, he ran for president on the Rhinoceros Party ticket. His candid dislike of Red Sox manager Don Zimmer may have made the difference between a division title and one of the most excruciating collapses in baseball history. Lee openly called Zimmer the "designated gerbil" and understandably earned the skipper's ire. Although Lee was a three-time seventeen-game winner and dominated in his appearances against the Yankees, Zimmer refused to start him in the catastrophic four-game series that the Yankees swept in Fenway to take the lead in the division race. While the fans were chanting "We want Lee!" Zimmer started rookie southpaw Bobby Sprowl in the final game, rather than the Spaceman. Sprowl lasted less than an inning, and the Yankees swept into first. Had the Red Sox won any one of the four games in that series, they would have won the division by two games.

Those who live by the wall must die by the wall.

ROGER ANGELL

Somehow the Sox fulfill the notion that we live in a fallen world.

A. BARTLETT GIAMATTI

Beyond the Fenway Fences, the trees of New England were tinged with reds and oranges. They might as well have been tears.

THOMAS BOSWELL

A Half-Game Heartbreak

In 1972, the players went out on strike in the spring, and many April games were canceled. When the dispute was resolved, the regular schedule began at the point where the strike ended. Games missed because of the strike were not rescheduled and were not played. As a consequence, teams ended the season with different totals of games played.

The Red Sox battled the Tigers for the division title to the last series of the season, three games between the rivals in Detroit. The Red Sox entered the series with a one-half game lead and needed to win two games to take the division title. During the first game of the series, the Red Sox faced Mickey Lolich, one of the most dominating pitchers in the American League. Early in the game, Carl Yastrzemski hit a ball over the centerfielder's head for an extra base hit. Yaz tried stretching the hit into a triple and should have done so easily. But Luis Aparicio, one of the greatest base runners in baseball history, was running the bases in front of Yastrzemski. Aparicio fell rounding third base and was forced to retreat back to the bag. Yastrzemski arrived at third with Aparicio standing on it. Yaz was called out for being the second of two runners on the same base. The play let Lolich off the hook, and the Red Sox lost the game. A loss the following day made the last game of the season academic. Boston won the finale, but lost the division by one-half game, because the Tigers played one more game than Boston did.

Ironically, the Tigers are also the only team to win a pennant by one-half game. Because rainouts were not rescheduled in 1908, the Tigers played one game less than the Indians and took the flag by one-half game, the only instance of any team ever having done so.

THE RED SOX

FANATIC

GREAT PROMISE CUT SHORT

Walt Dropo

In his rookie season of 1950, Walt Dropo, the pride of Moosup, Connecticut, hit .322, with 34 home runs and an astonishing 144 runs batted in, one short of Ted Williams's rookie record. His performance was so strong that he ousted Billy Goodman from first base, even though Goodman was having his career year. Goodman hit .354 and won the American League batting crown, but had to play five different positions to fit into the lineup. He has the distinction of being the only batting champion listed in the MacMillan encyclopedia as a utility player. Alas, Dropo's swing had a flaw.

[Boston manager] Joe [McCarthy] picked up [a weakness in Dropo's swing] right away. It couldn't be corrected and he knew it was just a matter of time before the rest of he league zoned in on it. They did the next year, and Walter was never the same hitter again. But in 1950, he sure was a terror.

RED SOX TEAMMATE

The next year, after his weakness had been exposed, Dropo's production dropped off the table, to a .239 average, with eleven home runs and fifty-seven RBIs in ninety-nine games. He played another eleven years with four other teams, hitting only 105 more round-trippers and ending with a .270 batting average. Dropo had been a major force in Boston's pennant contender in 1950, and the club's fortunes followed those of the Moose. The Red Sox would not contend for a pennant for another seventeen years.

Harry Agganis

Harry Agganis, the Golden Greek, grew up in Lynn, near Boston. He starred in baseball and as a football quarterback at Boston University.

[A] tall, handsome, clean-cut son of immigrant parents, a good student, an all-around athlete, a youth leader and a teen-age idol, Harry Agganis was the epitome of the American dream.

BRENDAN C. BOYD AND FRED C. HARRIS

When Agganis was drafted by the Cleveland Browns, it took a $25,000 bonus to lure him to Fenway. After only one season in the minors, Agganis made the Show as the Red Sox starting first baseman in 1954.

On June 6, 1955, when he was hitting .313, Agganis left the team in Kansas City, complaining of chest pain. He had pneumonia. Three weeks later, a massive pulmonary embolism lodged in his lungs and ended his life. He was twenty-five.

[H]e can't miss being a real good big leaguer. The pitching will fool him for a while, but he'll catch onto that like he has everything else about this game and then the Red Sox won't have to worry about first base for the next 10 years. I can tell you one more thing. If we ever need a fist down, I know our man.

PINKY HIGGINS

Tony Conigliaro

[T]he first time Conigliaro, who is a Boston boy, batted in Fenway Park he hit the first pitch out of Fenway Park, thus occasioning the greatest hoopla since the prodigal son came back and everybody in the place got half a day off.

FRANK DEFORD

Tony lived for the spotlight,
craved clutch situations, and
dreamed of being the hero . . .

DAVID CATANEO

Had he stayed healthy, without a doubt he would have hit 500 home runs playing in Fenway Park. He could hit home runs in that ballpark in his sleep.

CARL YASTRZEMSKI

Tony Conigliaro's meteoric ascent into greatness ended on August 17, 1967, when a ninety-mile-an-hour Jack Hamilton fastball hit him squarely in the left eye. Although he made two heroic attempts at a comeback, the damage to his vision could not be overcome, and he would never again be the formidable force he had been from his first swing at Fenway.

As soon as it crunched into me, it felt as if

the ball would go in my head and come out

the other side.

TONY CONIGLIARO

I knew it was bad. I dozed off for 20 minutes and when I woke up there was blood all over the sheets.

TONY CONIGLIARO

God, please, please don't let me die right here in the dirt at home plate at Fenway Park.

TONY CONIGLIARO

Fenway Brothers

Tony was not the only Conigliaro to play for Boston. His younger brother, Billy, another outfielder with a bit of pop in his bat, played with Tony on Red Sox teams for three years. There have been four other pairs of Red Sox brothers. Roy Johnson played in the Red Sox outfield from 1932 to 1935. Over his three full seasons in Boston he hit .316. His brother, "Indian Bob" Johnson, also an outfielder and one of the league's most feared sluggers in his prime, played for the Red Sox at the end of his career, in 1944 and 1945. Outfielder Cleo Carlyle played for the Red Sox in 1927. His brother, Dizzy Carlyle, again an outfielder, played for the Red Sox in 1925 and 1926. Hall of Fame catcher Rick Ferrell played for the Red Sox from 1933 to 1937. His brother, tall and tempestuous right-hander Wes Ferrell, won 25 games for the Red Sox in 1935. Ramon Martinez, brother of Pedro Martinez, pitched for Boston in 1999 and 2000.

THE RED SOX FANATIC

BACK TO THE HARDWOOD

On April 27, 1963, in Boston, Gene Conley, a center for the New York Knicks, faced Dave DeBusschere, who earned fame as a forward for the Detroit Pistons. There would be nothing remarkable about this confrontation were it not for the fact that the contest took place in Fenway Park. Gene Conley spent eleven years in the majors, including three in Boston, as a lanky right-handed pitcher. He recorded fifteen wins in one season and fourteen in another. In 1962 and 1963, DeBusschere made 32 appearances on the mound for the White Sox, ten as a starter. Conley and DeBusschere opposed each other during the fourth inning of the baseball game played on that date. Both players may have longed for the basketball court. In four innings, Conley walked six, surrendered four runs, all earned, and balked. DeBusschere yielded three runs, all earned, in two-thirds innings of relief, served up a home run to Frank Malzone, walked two, and threw a wild pitch. Boston won the game 9–5, but neither Conley nor DeBusschere were involved in the decision. The appearances by both pitchers were, alas, representative of their respective values to their teams. Nineteen sixty-three would be the last baseball season for both.

THE RED SOX FANATIC

THE IMPOSSIBLE DREAM

New England baseball fans would forever set their watches by the summer of '67. It was the year the Red Sox were reborn. For the first time since 1950 the team fielded a bona fide contender and a new generation got hooked on the Sox, and they were hooked for life.

DAVID CATANEO

It was a pennant race for the ages, with four teams still alive till the last Friday, and three fighting for the pennant on the final day.

BOB RYAN

Final Standings of the Clubs in 1966

AMERICAN LEAGUE

	W	L	PCT.	GB
Baltimore	97	62	.606	—
Minnesota	89	73	.549	9
Detroit	88	74	.545	10
Chicago	83	79	.512	12
Cleveland	81	81	.500	17
California	80	82	.494	18
Kansas City	74	86	.463	23
Washington	71	88	.447	25 1/2
Boston	72	90	.444	26
New York	70	89	.440	26 1/2

[Dick] Williams's 1967 Red Sox are not radically different in personnel from the 1966 bunch that plodded dismally to a ninth-place finish.

JOE JARES

Dick Williams took over as Red Sox skipper in 1967. Although he was a rookie manager, he immediately took charge.

There is one chief here—me—
and everyone else is an Indian.

DICK WILLIAMS, ANNOUNCING THAT CARL YASTRZEMSKI WOULD
NO LONGER BE TEAM CAPTAIN

I didn't want to be captain. I had my own problems. As the season got along I started to feel that I wasn't part of the team and that I was getting the cold shoulder. And every time someone had a gripe they came to me.

CARL YASTRZEMSKI

I can make you proud to be a baseball player.

And I can get rid of you and embarrass you.

You pick.

DICK WILLIAMS

The best Red Sox pitcher, Jim Lonborg, learned this year that he had to be "mean"— to brush back the hitters—and this helped him become a [22]-game winner.

WILLIAM LEGGETT

Impossible Dream Trivia Question 1

Who are the two players who were named Red Sox captain since Carl Yastrzemski?

Answer on page 344.

Turning the Season Around

The Red Sox lost their first game after the All-Star break in 1967, giving them a record of 42–40 on July 13. They then went on a tear that made them contenders. Against Baltimore, Detroit, and Cleveland they strung together ten wins in a row to go twelve games over .500 on July 23. The Red Sox began the streak in fifth place, six games out, and ended it in second place, a half game behind the White Sox.

[N]obody in sport in 1967 played any game with greater overall excellence, verve, and dedication than Carl Yastrzemski, no one excited the imagination more and no one carried out the dramatic promise that is inherent in every competitive sport more completely.

SPORTS ILLUSTRATED, NAMING CARL YASTRZEMSKI SPORTSMAN OF THE YEAR

In '67, I just completely changed my hitting style, from a straight away hitter and hitting the ball the opposite way to a dead-pull hitter.

CARL YASTRZEMSKI

I was never so sure of myself in my life.

CARL YASTRZEMSKI

About two months into the [1961] season, I was hitting .220 and was about ready to cry. . . . "I've got to talk to Ted," I said. . . . A day later, Ted showed up. . . . Ted stayed around two days and had me believing I could hit any pitcher. . . . From that point on, no matter the situation or any at-bat, no pressure ever bothered me again.

CARL YASTRZEMSKI

Double-duty Reggie

The Red Sox began the 1967 season with Mike Andrews, their young second baseman, hobbled by an injury. Dick Williams shifted Reggie Smith, a Gold Glove–caliber centerfielder, to second. Reggie played six games at second, making one error at the position, before Andrews took over on an everyday basis April 21. Those six games would be the only time Smith would play second base in his career.

Answer to Impossible Dream Trivia Question 1

Jim Rice became Red Sox captain in 1985. Jason Varitek was named captain in 2005.

Don't you ever let anyone
monkey with your swing.

TED WILLIAMS, TO THE YOUNG CARL YASTRZEMSKI

Carl Yastrzemski kept his skills sharp by playing his position during batting practice and by having batting coach Walt Hriniak hit fungoes off The Wall before batting practice had ever started.

GEORGE V. HIGGINS

I've never watched a player have the kind of year he had and that was in 1967 with Carl Yastrzemski. . . . I played with some good players on that Brooklyn club, Jackie Robinson and Pee Wee Reese and Hodges and Campanella and all those guys, Snider . . . but I've never watched a player having one complete year like Yastrzemski had.

DICK WILLIAMS

The Perfect Player

Carl Yastrzemski won seven Gold Gloves in his career. He is considered by many to be the best defensive leftfielder the American League produced since Hall of Famer Al Simmons in the 1930s. Yastrzemski's great all-round performance in 1967 inspired Dick Williams to call him "the perfect player."

Yazsir that's my baby.

He lived, breathed, ate, and slept baseball. If he went 0-for-4, he couldn't live with it. He could live with himself, if he went 1-for-3. He was happy if he went 2-for-4. That's the way the man suffered.

JOE LAHOUD

It is obviously impossible for one man to win a pennant. And yet if it had ever been done it was done in 1967, and the man who did it was Boston left-fielder Carl Yastrzemski.

LAWRENCE RITTER AND DONALD HONIG

A Clutch Performance for the Ages

During the last two weeks of the 1967 season, Carl Yastrzemski dismantled the league almost single-handedly. Tony Conigliaro, the young Red Sox cleanup hitter, a talent some, including Johnny Pesky, thought was in a class with Joe DiMaggio, had taken a fastball to the face and was out of baseball until 1969. Yastrzemski took charge and produced enough offense for two. Over the last twelve games of the season, Yaz hit (not slugged) .523, with five home runs and fourteen runs batted in. In the deciding two-game season finale against the Twins, Yastrzemski went 7 for 8, hit a home run in the first game and put the Red Sox ahead in the second and deciding game.

In voting for Yastrzemski [as the league's best player in 1967], the players revealed their own illiteracy. Written in were such entries as Yaztremski, Yastremski, Yastrezemski, Yastreszski, Yastremzminski, Yaststrenski, and Yazstremenski. One player, obviously consulting a boxscore, voted for Y'str'mski, while several others opted for the safe designation "Yaz—Boston."

DANIEL OKRENT

The Impossible Dream Trivia
Question 2

Why did Carl Yastrzemski reject the trophy that was offered to him for winning the Triple Crown in 1967?

Answer on page 356.

Beyond the Triple Crown

In addition to posting a league-high batting average of .326, driving in the most runs with 121, and tying Harmon Killebrew for the home run crown with 44, in 1967, Yaz led the league in hits with 189, slugging percentage at .622, total bases with 360, and runs scored with 112.

Answer to The Impossible Dream Trivia Question 2

Yastrzemski's name was misspelled. The spelling was never corrected, and Yaz never accepted the trophy. The Triple Crown trophy is owned by a private collector.

O give us the strength of Hercules, the courage of David, the wisdom of Pericles, the luck that has helped bring us this far, to the edge of paradise, to the golden halyard that raises the pennant. Let the little round ball on the wheel of fortune drop for us and not the Twins.

HAROLD KAESE

[N]ot infrequently in baseball the worm turns in the waning moments.

IRVING VAUGHN

In bullfighting, I understand that the moment of truth usually comes sometime around four in the afternoon. I have a feeling that it will come a lot earlier today.

CAL ERMER, TWINS MANAGER, ON THE GAME AT FENWAY, OCTOBER 1, 1967

Yaz described the moment he tied the score in the season finale.

Sure enough he came in with that sinker that started to tail away. Except I knew just where it was headed and I drilled it to center for a single that scored two runs.

CARL YASTRZEMSKI

Fans poured out of the bleachers, grandstand, and box seats and covered the infield with a mob of squirming, dancing, jumping humanity . . . Frenzied celebrants ripped pieces off the left-field scoreboard, pulled up swatches of the hallowed turf, climbed the screen behind home plate and pounded on the dugout.

DAVID CATANEO

Living the Impossible Dream

The 1967 pennant race was the most hair-raising in American League history. Four teams were within a game and a half of the top with four games to go. The Twins had won their only pennant two years earlier, but the other three teams had suffered prolonged championship droughts. The pitching-rich White Sox had taken the flag eight years earlier, but it was the only championship they had won in four decades. The Tigers hadn't been to the World Series for twenty-two years, the Red Sox for twenty-one.

The White Sox were the first to be eliminated, bowing out on Friday, September 29, after suffering losses to the lowly Senators and Athletics. Minnesota, the team with the best balance of hitting and pitching, came into Fenway for the final two games of the season with a one-game lead over the Red Sox and Tigers. The Red Sox had to win both games to take the flag. The Tigers were still breathing fire, tied with the Red Sox and facing the Angels in four games, two consecutive doubleheaders needed to make up rainouts.

Boston, behind the arm of Jose Santiago and three hits from Carl Yastrzemski, took the first game against the Twins, 6–4 on Saturday, September 30. Yaz slugged home run number forty-four, to tie him with Minnesota's hulking Harmon Killebrew, a monstrous home-run hitter, who would retire fourth on the all-time list. The Tigers split the first doubleheader to remain one game back.

The game between the Red Sox and Twins on Sunday, October 1, would bring one team to the top. The other team would be eliminated. Detroit could force a tie for the flag by sweeping the Angels in the doubleheader.

The Red Sox–Twins game was a battle of twenty-game winners. Dean Chance, Cy Young Award winner in 1964, entered the day 20–13. He had already beaten Boston four times without a loss, including a five-inning, rain-shortened no-hitter against the Red Sox on August 6. Jim Lonborg was 21–9 for Boston, but hadn't beaten the Twins in three tries.

The Twins had Tony Oliva, one of the premier hitters in baseball, slugging outfielder Bob Allison, and the young Rod Carew in their lineup. The Red Sox had the Cardiac Kids, so-called because of their habit of coming back to win tight games late. George Scott, Reggie Smith, and Joe Foy provided punch at the plate. The great young talent, rightfielder, and cleanup hitter Tony Conigliaro, had been felled by a beanball on August 18, out for the season and never to recover the level of play that could have led him to the Hall of Fame. But the Red Sox had Yaz, the best defensive leftfielder in the American League since the 1930s, and on a Triple Crown pace at the plate. Yaz rose to dizzying new levels in the clutch. He had gone 3 for 4 on Saturday.

The Twins grabbed the lead in the first inning, 2–0, on errors by George Scott and, of all people, Yaz. The score remained the same through five, and Jim Lonborg was scheduled to bat first in the Boston sixth. The conventional move is to hit for your starter if your team trails after five innings. Dick Williams ignored convention and let Lonborg lead off. Lonborg laid a bunt down the third-base line and beat it out. Singles by super subs Jerry

Adair and Dalton Jones loaded the bases. Yastrzemski stepped in. He had seen Chance's sinker and knew that it broke away from a left-handed hitter. Chance threw the sinker as the second pitch. It came toward Yaz inside, but he knew it would break over the plate. It did, and Yaz hit it into centerfield, scoring Lonborg and Adair to tie the game. Ken Harrelson, an outfielder Boston had acquired to replace the injured Tony C., batted next. He would have a big year in 1968, but he was yet to produce big numbers for Boston. On a three-and-two pitch, Harrelson hit a grounder to shortstop Zoilo Versalles, a former league MVP. Versalles threw home, but Dalton Jones scored ahead of the throw. Al Worthington, a veteran right-hander, replaced Chance, only to throw two wild pitches. Yastrzemski scored, and the Red Sox led 4–2. An error by Killebrew at first allowed Harrelson to score the fifth run.

The Twins threatened in the eighth, putting runners on first and second, with two out. Bob Allison hit a ball into the leftfield corner, a sure double in most parks. But Yaz fired a seed to second, cutting Allison down and limiting the Minnesota rally to one run.

Lonborg induced a double-play ball to end a mild threat in the ninth and pitched a complete game to beat the Twins for the only time that year. He earned his twenty-second win and the Cy Young Award. Yaz had gone four for four, seven of eight in the final two games. Minnesota was eliminated. The Red Sox were on top of the standings. The stands emptied and thousands of fans flooded the field.

But Detroit had won the first game of their second doubleheader in two days. The Red Sox radio network carried the game after the thriller with the Twins had ended. Trailing by three in the ninth, the Tigers mounted a rally. Dick McAuliffe, the fleet Detroit second baseman, however, hit into a season-ending double play. Detroit fans were so stunned, they refused to leave the stadium. Only after the lights were turned off in Tiger Stadium did the heartbroken throng file into the streets.

The Red Sox fell in the World Series, 4 games to 3, but the Impossible Dream was real. The team had risen from ninth place in 1966, twenty-six games out, to capture the pennant in the wildest finish in major league history.

The Impossible Dream Trivia
Question 3

How many double plays did Dick McAuliffe hit into in 1967?

Answer on page 372.

The Relentless Competitor

After Game 1 of the 1967 World Series, Carl Yastrzemski took extra batting practice. In Game 2, Yaz hit two home runs, one of them off Cardinal right-hander Dick Hughes, and drove in four runs. Jim Lonborg pitched a one-hit shutout and the Red Sox won 5–0. Yaz would also homer against Hughes in Game 6.

What a great thing it is to play in a World Series. I'd say the only problem with it is that we have 20 relatives and friends staying at our house and it's a little difficult getting into the bathroom.

CARL YASTRZEMSKI

Karl Marx, who said that religion was the [people's] opiate, would have revised himself had he watched the Red Sox unite to throw off their ninth-place chains. The Red Sox are the opiate right now, Karl, baby . . .

BUD COLLINS

We're not going to be able to fathom the year until we sit beside a winter fireplace. We should have dinner together and drink some fine wine, and maybe we will. Then we can sit across the table from each other and shake our heads.

JIM LONBORG

Yaz in the Field

Carl Yastrzemski is known as the leftfielder who replaced Ted Williams. He played leftfield in Boston, of course, beginning in 1961, the year after the Splendid Splinter retired. He played three other positions for the Red Sox, however. He played first base during fourteen seasons. In six of those seasons, first base was his primary position. In 1964, Yaz was the Red Sox centerfielder. He served as the Red Sox DH more than 350 times late in his career. In 1964 and 1973, Yaz played a total of thirty-three games at third base.

Answer to The Impossible Dream Trivia Question 3

Dick McAuliffe hit into two double plays in 1967.

A Penny Saved

Buddy LeRoux was the Red Sox trainer from 1966 to 1974. In that capacity, he earned a World Series share in 1967. LeRoux invested his share so successfully that, with Red Sox Vice President for Player Development Haywood Sullivan, he headed a syndicate that bought the team from the estate of Tom Yawkey in 1977.

Off-season Conditioning

On December 24, 1967, during a ski tour that extended from Vermont to California, Jim Lonborg failed to execute a snowplow maneuver properly at Lake Tahoe and tore a ligament in his knee. He would make 16 fewer starts in 1968 than he did in 1967. His record would go from 22–9 to 6–10.

There is utterly no significance in the fact that Red Sox pitcher Jim Lonborg . . . tore a cartilage skiing at a California resort operated by Harmon Killebrew's cousin.

SHIRLEY POVICH

Final Standings of the Clubs in 1967

AMERICAN LEAGUE

	W	L	PCT.	GB
Boston	92	70	.565	—
Detroit	91	71	.562	1
Minnesota	91	71	.562	1
Chicago	89	73	.549	3
California	84	77	.522	7 1/2
Baltimore	76	85	.472	15 1/2
Washington	76	85	.472	15 1/2
Cleveland	75	87	.463	17
New York	72	90	.444	20
Kansas City	62	99	.385	29 1/2

Bill Clinton will fall again, Richard Nixon rise again, and Jupiter align with Mars; Newt Gingrich may become a social worker . . . Billy Graham might become a rabbi and Madonna a nun; Peter Rose may scream apologia, Bob Uecker find the front row, and National League return to Boston—all this will occur before baseball knows a finer hour than nineteen hundred and sixty-seven.

CURT SMITH

A Day at the Orifice

After fifteen seasons and 157 wins in the Big Leagues, Jim Lonborg retired to Scituate and became a dentist.

THE RED SOX FANATIC

A TALE OF TWO TRADES

Whatever his team, Oakland, the White Sox, or the Yankees, Danny Cater always tore up the park on his visits to Fenway, spraying hits and bouncing balls off the Green Monster all series long. Through 1971, Cater hadn't had a weak season, hitting .290 or higher in three years. In his worst year, he hit .262. In 1968, he finished second to Carl Yastrzemski in the race for the batting title. More important, Cater knew how to make his hits count. In 1970 in New York, he hit only six home runs, but batted .301 and drove in seventy-six runs, fifty of which came against Boston, or so it seemed.

After the 1971 season, the Red Sox dealt left-handed reliever Sparky Lyle to the Yankees for Cater. Lyle had respectable numbers in Boston, but Fenway and the Wall are notoriously tough on southpaws. It looked like a great trade. But, as soon as Cater made Fenway his home, the numbers plummeted. In 1972, his first year in Boston, he hit .237 and, in ninety-two games, drove in exactly thirty-nine runs. His performance improved in a part-time role the next year, a .313 average, but again, in sixty-three games, he managed a meager twenty-four RBIs. After a

.246 campaign, he was shipped to St. Louis, his final destination, in 1975.

In the meantime, Sparky Lyle became a sensation in the Bronx. Yankee Stadium and its cavernous leftfield, particularly before its renovation, fostered the careers of some dominating left-handers: Herb Pennock, Lefty Gomez, Whitey Ford, Ron Guidry. Lyle learned to play the park and joined the Yankee elite. When he entered the game at home, the organist played "Pomp and Circumstance." In his first three years in pinstripes, he recorded ERAs between 1.66 and 2.51. In only one year did his ERA rise above 3.13. He earned World Series rings in 1977 and 1978. You should choose your trading partners with care. If you sup with the devil, after all, you must expect wind.

It was the worst trade I ever made.

DICK O'CONNELL, RED SOX GM

The flip side happened in 1997, when the Red Sox sent an All-Star to the West Coast for two unknowns. The trade became the steal of the decade. Reliever Heathcliff Slocumb was named to the All-Star team in 1995. In 1996, he went 5–5 for the Red Sox with a respectable 3.02 ERA. In 1997, he was 0–5 with an ERA over 5.00 in Boston. At the trading deadline in 1997, the Red Sox suddenly dealt Slocumb to Seattle for two players with twenty games of major league experience between them. Slocumb went 2–5 with a 5.32 ERA, while earning $3 million with the Mariners in 1998. He bounced around among three teams in 1999 and 2000, recording a 2–4 mark and registering ERAs as high as double figures. The two players who came to Fenway earned combined salaries of $342,000 in 1998, but their pay would rise dramatically. The position player the Red Sox acquired hadn't played a game in the big leagues, but became Boston's regular backstop in 1999 and one of the greatest leaders and clutch players the franchise had ever known. In 2005, Jason Varitek would win a Gold Glove and serve as only the third Red Sox captain in over 80 years. The other was a right-handed pitcher with a record of 2–4 and an ERA of 6.96 in

Seattle. Derek Lowe would first serve as a stalwart and a closer in the Boston bullpen. He would win twenty-one games as a starter in 2002 and seventeen more in 2003. In 2004, he would win the deciding games in all three Red Sox post-season series. The bottom line on the deal: one All-Star for one World Series ring.

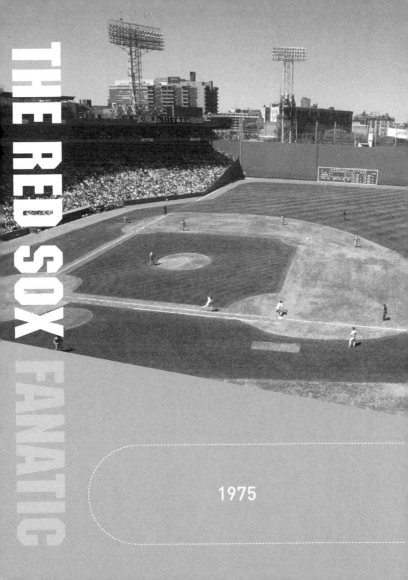

THE RED SOX FANATIC

1975

Carlton Fisk

Granite-tough, he asked no quarter and certainly gave none. . . . He was demanding of those around him and even more demanding of himself. But above all he was a pro's pro. And he was that way from the start.

WARREN N. WILBERT

Looe-Eee

If a man put a gun to my head and said I'm going to pull the trigger if you lose this game, I'd want Luis Tiant to pitch that game.

DARRELL JOHNSON

He has six pitches and he throws them from all angles.

REDS SCOUTING REPORT ON LUIS TIANT

He showed them just a piece of the ball like a guy flashing French postcards. . . . Luis on the mound studied the heavens, the centerfield bleachers, every blade of God's green grass. He threw the ball with his back to the batter. He threw it from a crouch. He threw it with a little jump. He had so much motion on the mound that his ball seemed to come out of a crowd scene.

JIM MURRAY

I didn't do it [his unusual windup] for show. I did it to get batters out. Players would tell me, "We can't tell where the ball is coming from."

LUIS TIANT

I gave him [Frank Howard] shoulder, back, foot and the ball last.

LUIS TIANT

He threw everything at me but the ball.

FRANK HOWARD

The first is the step-by-step drop of his hands . . . Second, his rhythm in the way he drops his hands has to be constant and, after the way everybody in the American League complained, he's been okay there. Third, if he throws to first, he'd better look like he stepped to first before he threw.

FRED FLEIG, NATIONAL LEAGUE SUPERVISOR OF UMPIRES, ON TIANT AND THE BALK RULE

When I'm in Boston, I always feel like I'm home. I almost cry, I feel so good.

LUIS TIANT

The Spaceman

"He is," many say "a typical left-hander." Not really. Bill Lee is not a typical anything. Bill Lee is an original.

DAVE ANDERSON, *NEW YORK TIMES*

I believe in what Harry Truman said,
what Voltaire said, that I'll fight to the
death for my right to say what I want.

BILL LEE

Voltaire?

A LISTENER

Harry Voltaire, he had 40 consecutive hits, he was in the top 40 in Paris.

BILL LEE

Tell [American League President Joe] Cronin I threw a spitter in Detroit a while back. Tony Taylor hit it into the upper deck. . . . Hell, if K-Y jelly went off the market the California Angels' whole staff would be out of baseball or pitching in Pittsfield. Yes, I have a tube of K-Y petroleum in my locker. . . . So tell Cronin he'd better fine me because I was a bad boy.

BILL LEE

When the Iranians were holding our embassy people captive, instead of the Marines we should have sent Burleson and Petrocelli over there. They would have come back in 48 hours with the hostages, the ayatollah and a couple of million barrels of oil.

BILL LEE

They call him the Spaceman. Well don't kid yourself. Bill Lee knows exactly what he's doing all the time. He got the reputation he wanted. He worked at it.

REGGIE SMITH

Fred Lynn

If I could be bigger and stronger and maybe run into a few less walls and not pay the price for what I did, that would be great. But I would not compromise my style.

FRED LYNN

[I] don't get enjoyment out of being the center of attention. I get my enjoyment between the lines of the ballfield and at home.

FRED LYNN, ON BEING NAMED ROOKIE OF THE YEAR

Two-sport Star

Fred Lynn played defensive back on the University of Southern California football team.

The League Championship Series

We were a strong club, but there's no doubt that it was the year of the Red Sox. They couldn't do anything wrong. Yaz was the perfect player at that time.

REGGIE JACKSON

A Rookie Season Like No Other

In 1975, Fred Lynn's rookie season, the Red Sox center-fielder led the league in runs scored with 103 and doubles with 47. His .331 batting average and 105 runs batted in were second in the league. He was also fifth in triples, sixth in hits, and sixteenth in home runs. His play in the field was reckless and sensational. Lynn, of course, won the Rookie of the Year award by a vote that would have been unanimous, except for a half vote garnered by fellow Gold Dust Twin, Jim Rice. But the most remarkable accolade Lynn earned in 1975 was the Most Valuable Player award. Not only was Lynn the first rookie to win the league's top honor, he won it by a record margin. The only two first-place votes Lynn did not capture went to Oakland's Hall of Fame closer, Rollie Fingers. Lynn's success didn't exactly go to his head, however.

Fred Lynn's freshman season in the Bigs was one of titanic achievement. When the last hit had been made and the last out recorded for his 1975 Rookie of the Year season, it went down as the greatest rookie season in Red Sox history . . .

WARREN N. WILBERT

In the second game [of the ALCS], Oakland's Sal Bando slammed four successive shots off the left field wall—all of which might have been home runs in any other park in the majors. Left fielder Carl Yastrzemski, a virtuoso performer of the Wall, twice held Bando to a single, and in one case cut down Bert Campaneris attempting to advance from first to third on Bando's hit.

PHILIP H. BESS

The World Series

Resolved, that the Senate of the United States recognizes the quality of excellence of both of these great teams, wishes both teams well and hopes that the home team be victorious in each game of the World Series.

SENATE RESOLUTION, INTRODUCED BY SENATOR EDWARD KENNEDY OF MASSACHUSETTS

The Red Sox, of course, had the home-field advantage. In an act of dubious loyalty to the Reds, Senator John Glenn of Ohio voted in favor of the resolution.

A Rice-less Postseason

On September 23, in Detroit, Vern Ruhle hit the rookie Jim Rice with a pitch and broke his hand. As a consequence, Rice missed the entire postseason. At the time of his injury, Rice was hitting .309, with twenty-two home runs and 102 RBIs.

The Reds were prohibitive favorites. They had an overpowering offense, packed from top to bottom with high averages, power and speed. Their defense and bullpen were first rate. The Big Red Machine had won pennants in 1970 and 1972 and the division in 1973, but had not won a World Championship. The 1975 and 1976 teams were the best of the crop.

Boston will surprise everyone,
the Reds too.

TONY BLACKWELL

Game 1

Luis Tiant shut out the powerful Reds and survived one surprise from Rick Colosi.

With Johnny Bench, the dangerous one, at the plate, Looie still concentrated on Morgan. His next pickoff attempt saw Morgan waved free to second base because Umpire Rick Colosi detected a deceptive "double dip" of Tiant's knee.

DAVID CONDON, *CHICAGO TRIBUNE*, ON GAME 1

The balk had no effect on the outcome of Game 1. Tiant shut out Cincinnati and even got a six-run inning going with a leadoff base hit in the seventh inning.

Hobbies of the Rich and Famous

Fred Lynn and Ted Williams shared the same passion off the field. Both loved fishing. Some commentators believe that Ted Williams may have been as great with a rod as with a bat. Lynn retreated to fresh-water fishing after the 1975 World Series.

I honestly believe he loves fishing more than baseball. Baseball gives him an opportunity to fish in the off-season.

DEE DEE, MRS. FRED LYNN

Ghost balls, junk balls, spirit balls. What did Looie Tiant throw today? He threw a handful of sand into the gears of the Big Red Machine.

BUCK CANAL, SPANISH LANGUAGE RADIO ANNOUNCER

Game 3

After being shut out in Game 1, the Reds rallied for two runs in the ninth inning of Game 2 to gain a split in Boston. Game 3 was, therefore, pivotal. The Series was acquiring its shape. Game 3 would assign the favorite and underdog roles to each team. The 1975 Series was great, not just for Game 6, but for the resurgence of both teams, for four games with amazing comebacks. One of those comebacks took place in Game 3. Because of Ed Armbrister, the Red Sox comeback in Game 3 ultimately fell short.

The Red Sox fell behind 5–1 in the fifth. But they came back. One run came in the seventh inning on the first of two pinch-hit homers in the Series by, of all things, a former Cincinnati first-round draft choice. The Red Sox had acquired outfielder Bernie Carbo from the Cardinals before the 1974 season. Carbo had been taken ahead of Johnny Bench in the 1965 draft. The two had played together on the Reds from 1969 until 1972. Bench must have mouthed off to Carbo when he came up to pinch-hit, to "psyche him out" in the parlance of the day, because Carbo lit into Bench visibly and verbally as he crossed the plate after sending the ball over the fence. With a Boston run in the sixth and two more runs on another home run in the ninth, Game 3 became the second in a series of nail-biters. The Reds failed to score in the bottom of the ninth, and the game went into extra innings.

The Red Sox went down without a run in the top of the tenth. Fleet Reds centerfielder Cesar Geronimo led off the Cincinnati frame with a single. Enter Ed Armbrister, diminutive reserve outfielder and adept bunter, stage right. Armbrister laid down a bunt in front of home plate. When Carlton Fisk attempted to field the bunt, Armbrister collided with him, and Fisk threw wildly to second base, trying to nail the advancing Geronimo. The Red Sox screamed for an interference call. The umpire, Larry Barnett, denied the request, ruling that Armbrister's interference was unintentional.

Now, when a batter runs toward first to the left of the foul line and blocks the catcher's throw to first, the umpire doesn't ask the batter if he obstructed the throw on purpose, before calling him out. There is no intent requirement, in other words. When a batter hinders a catcher in fielding a dropped third strike, there is no intent requirement for the batter to be called out. When a batter collides with a catcher attempting to field a ball in extra innings in a World Series game, it seems, there is an intent requirement. Or is there? Let's look at the rules.

In 1975, Baseball Rule 6.06 provided:

A batter is out for illegal action when . . .

He interferes with the catcher's fielding or throwing by step-ping out of the batter's box or making any other movement that hinders the catcher's play at home base.

Rule 7.09 provided:

It is interference by a batter or runner when . . .

He fails to avoid a fielder who is attempting to field the ball, or intentionally interferes with a thrown ball . . .

Pursuant to Rule 2.00, the term "fielder" included the catcher.

Rule 6.06 didn't say, "intentionally interferes." It had no intent requirement. Rule 7.09 contains an intent requirement for interference with a ball once it has been thrown, but not for interfering with a fielder attempting to field the ball.

Other baseball rules contain intent requirements. It depends on the specific situation. When a batter deflects a batted ball (Rule 605(i)), or when a base runner interferes with a batted ball by dropping his helmet (Commentary to Rule 605(h)), the player is out only when the action is deliberate. There was no requirement in the 1975 version of Rule 606(c) that obstructing the catcher need be deliberate to constitute interference, when the ball is hit into fair territory.

Nevertheless, Barnett applied an intent requirement in the bottom of the tenth inning in Game 3 of the World Series. As a result of Fisk's errant throw, Geronimo advanced to third and Armbrister to second. An out later, Joe Morgan's fly ball over a drawn-in outfield drove in the deciding run.

Imagine, if you will, two scenarios. In the first, Fisk tags Armbrister out and, unobstructed, fires to second to nip Geronimo for a double play. The inning is over. In the second, Armbrister had been called out for interference and Geronimo had been sent back to first. As in the actual game, Merv Rettenmund, the batter preceding Morgan, is retired for the second out. The outfield is at normal depth. The ball Morgan hit becomes a routine fly for out number three, and no runs score. With the game extended to eleven innings or more, the Red Sox manage to prevail. How dramatic would Fisk's blast off the foul pole in Game 6 have been then?

Replays showed Armbrister was guilty of standing transfixed for perhaps a second or two while Fisk desperately was floundering for the ball.

RICHARD DOZER, *CHICAGO TRIBUNE*

It was simply a collision. It is interference only when the batter intentionally gets in the way of the fielder. I signaled that the ball was fair and in play.

LARRY BARNETT

. . . I probably tagged [Armbrister] pushing him out of the way . . . It might as well be the Cincinnati Bengals out there playing the Patriots.

CARLTON FISK

We lose the game. Reds one. Red Sox one, umpire one.

JIM WILLOUGHBY

If I'd been the manager, I'd have bit his ear off; I'd a Van Goghed him.

BILL LEE

Game 4

Game 4 saw another amazing performance by the ageless Luis Tiant, a complete-game, 163-pitch, one-run victory.

Although the Reds had Tiant on the ropes early, the veteran American Leaguer refused to quit. As the game progressed, Tiant grew stronger and stronger.

THOMAS BOSWELL

My control wasn't as sharp like in Boston. My breaking ball wasn't as good as in Boston. I had to go with my fastball most of the time. I wanted to stay in the game and finish the game. Last year Darrell Johnson have confidence in me. Every tough game he know I going to do the job. I glad he left me in.

LUIS TIANT

Will you be ready for Sunday?

REPORTER

I not too tired tonight. I make 180 pitches sometimes.

LUIS TIANT

Game 6

Game 6 of the 1975 World Series is one of the greatest World Series games ever played. The Red Sox grabbed a three-run lead in the first inning on Fred Lynn's home run, but fell behind by three after seven and a half. Bernie Carbo, former Reds number-one draft choice, pinch-hit in the bottom of the eighth with two runners on board and parked a Rawley Eastwick pitch in the centerfield bleachers. It was his second pinch-hit home run against his former teammates in the Series.

I'm heading for second base and I see the ball land in the bleachers. Now I round second base and I'm looking at Pete Rose and I'm yelling at him, "Don't you wish you were this strong?" and Rose is yelling back, "Isn't this fun?"

BERNIE CARBO

The greatest dramatics, though, began in the bottom of the ninth. The Red Sox loaded the bases with none out. Speedy Boston second baseman Denny Doyle was on third, when Fred Lynn came up to bat. On the first pitch, Lynn lofted a fly ball down the leftfield line. Reds left-fielder George Foster had an average arm, clearly the weakest arm in an outfield with strong, accurate throwers. Foster caught the ball virtually on top of the foul line, about 40 feet past third base. Doyle broke for home. It would take a perfect throw to catch Doyle. Foster threw a strike, on one bounce to the plate, and Johnny Bench's swipe tag nipped Doyle. The game film suggests that third-base coach Don Zimmer gave Doyle the green light, but opinions differ on that point.

Lynn Meets the Wall

In the fifth inning of Game 6, Fred Lynn, chasing a drive by Ken Griffey Sr., ran full speed to the wall at the juncture of the left- and centerfield sections. He spun around and slammed backward into the wall, fell to the ground, and lay in a heap for several minutes. He managed to avoid serious injury, but Tom Yawkey padded the wall before the 1976 season because of the near disaster with Lynn. The news delighted Fred Lynn.

I'll run into that wall all day now.

FRED LYNN

Fred popped it up, behind third, maybe 80 feet down the line. Foster ran in and had an easy catch. Zimmer, the third base coach, shouted to Doyle on third, "No, No!" But Denny, of course, thought Zim was saying "Go!" He was out by half a mile.

CARL YASTRZEMSKI

The game went into extra innings for even more spectacular heroics.

I'm going to hit one off the wall and it's up to you to bring me home.

CARLTON FISK TO FRED LYNN, BEFORE HIS AT-BAT LEADING OFF
THE TWELFTH INNING OF GAME 6

There's a long drive. If it stays fair . . . Home run! We will have a seventh game in this 1975 World Series. . . . And Carlton Fisk had a lot of little boy in him right there, Joe.

DICK STOCKTON

That was the greatest moment of my life—after my two kids.

CARLTON FISK

As a 10-year-old during Game 6 in '75 I threw up after the Fisk HR in jubilation.

SHERMAN ROBBINS

A History-making Day at the Office

In the eleventh inning, Dwight Evans caught a scorcher off the bat of Joe Morgan, in deep rightfield, on the warning track at the left end of the grandstands. Evans then threw to first base for a double play. Without the catch, there would have been no tie in the twelfth inning and no walk-off home run by Carlton Fisk. When interviewed about the catch after the game, Evans said, "That's what they pay me to do."

Game 6 in Boston was a landmark World Series game. In the future it will go down with the Dean boys' World Series, the 1926 Yankees-Cardinals, the 1946 Boston–St. Louis, to name a few.

JIM MURRAY

So now the series is tied, three games to three, and, as best we can calculate at this hour, the next team to win will have a distinct advantage.

CHARLES MAHER

Red Sox fans act like they won the World Series in 1975.

MARTY BRENNAMAN, REDS RADIO BROADCASTER

We, the Red Sox, won that World Series, 3 games to 4.

CARLTON FISK

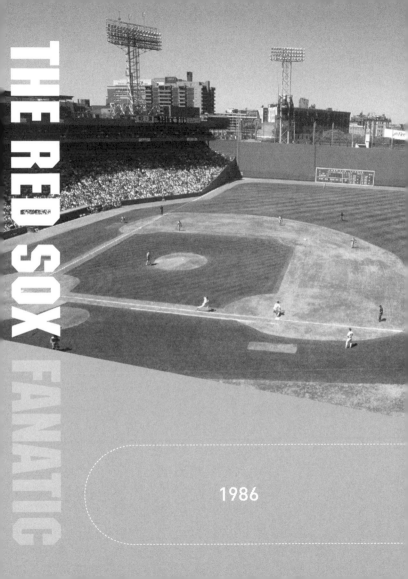

THE RED SOX

FANATIC

1986

A Sweet and Scholarly Revenge

The Angels had been very successful pitching to Marty Barrett during the 1986 regular season. A little homework turned the tables on California in the playoffs. Barrett watched videotape of all his at bats against the Angels that year to see just how California pitchers had gotten him out. Marty figured the Angels would go with what worked against him in the regular season. He was right. He looked for the same pitches the Angels pitchers had thrown in the same situations during the regular season, got them, and hit .367 in the ALCS.

Spike Owen

As far as ideal shortstops go, Owen is not going to meet many of the criteria—but he grows on you. . . . He is not a shortstop a team builds around, like an Alan Trammell or Ozzie Smith. . . . Owen has been honest with himself and doesn't try to do things that are out of reach.

THE SCOUTING REPORT: 1986

Spike Owen is, beyond any possible doubt, the best defensive shortstop in the American League. He is as overwhelmingly good at the art of catching batted balls and turning them into outs as Don Mattingly is at hitting pitched balls.

THE GREAT AMERICAN STAT BOOK

Wade Boggs

Boggs broke in with a .349 batting average, soon to look like an off-year for him.

DONALD HONIG

No Relation to Clete Boyer

Spike Owen's actual given name is Spike. Not only that, but you can tell your friends that the "D" in Spike D. Owen stands for Dee.

When it comes to hitting, Wade Boggs doesn't have a weakness . . . Boggs read Ted Williams' book when he was a youngster and it has been his guide ever since. He rarely swings at a pitch out of the strike zone, and he watches the ball through its entire flight to the instant it lands in the catcher's mitt.

THE SCOUTING REPORT: 1986

Bogg's batting tactics are similar to Ted Williams's—wait for the pitch . . . then hit it. Boggs commits on a pitch very late so, unlike Williams, he rarely pulls the ball.

DAVID PINTO

I used to tell my pitchers I could get them two strikes on Boggs easy, but from then on they were on their own. There's no doubt in my mind that he is the best two-strike hitter in history.

RENE LACHEMANN

A woman will be elected
president before Wade Boggs is
called out on strikes.

GEORGE BRETT

A Brilliant Consistency

Wade Boggs is the only twentieth-century player to have seven consecutive 200-hit seasons.

Ted Williams' discipline at the plate resulted in high walk totals, which, in turn, reduced the number of hits he got. He may not have committed to swinging at as many pitches as players with higher hit totals, but when he swung, he chose a good pitch. Only five players had higher career averages than he did, but Ted Williams never collected 200 hits in a single season. His highest hit total was 193, in 1940.

Unimpressive defensively when he reached the major leagues, Wade Boggs worked hard to improve his fielding and become one of the better third basemen in the American League. The gold standard for third basemen since World War II and to some, before, is the Orioles' Brooks Robinson. His plays against the Reds in the 1970 World Series are legendary. By playing one of the best, possibly the best hot corners ever, Robinson earned the title "The Human Vacuum Cleaner."

Heretofore uncelebrated as a fielder, Boggs has been semi-Brooksian at third base: if not a Hoover, at least a Dust Buster.

TONY KORNHEISER

Was That Crystal Ball a Two-Seamer or a Four-Seamer?

When Roger Clemens had pitched in only two injury-shortened seasons and had compiled a career record of 16–9, Bill James wrote an article in his *Baseball Abstract* about isolated, single achievements as an indicator of major league talent. James noted that Clemens had once struck out sixteen batters in a major league game without walking anyone. James considered the implications of this single outing and offered a projection. Of the then completely unproven, injury-plagued twenty-three-year-old, James predicted: Roger Clemens will be a great pitcher.

Roger Clemens

I am intense, no question about it. Every time I toe the rubber it's no different for me than it was in the World Series.

ROGER CLEMENS

[P]layers like Roger Clemens now keep books on the umpires. Clemens can identify which umpires call strikes on high or low pitches, which ones have a wide strike zone and which ones will squeeze the plate.

JOE MORGAN

Roger Clemens has been touted as the Red Sox' best pitching prospect in many, many years, but he was hampered by an injury last season for the second year in a row. When he is healthy, Clemens is the hardest thrower in the league and has the ability to be a twenty-five-game winner.

* * *

OVERALL:

If. If. If.

When? When? When?

THE SCOUTING REPORT: 1986

Now! Now! Now!

Roger Clemens's career year was 1986. He led the league in wins (twenty-four), winning percentage (.857), and earned run average (2.54). One of his four losses was by a score of 1–0, the sole run resulting from his own error. On April 29, Rocket Roger struck out twenty Seattle Mariners. Clemens led the league in strikeouts for most of the season. In his last start, however, he was hit by a batted ball, and left the game early with a total of 238 Ks on the year. The Angels' ace, Mark Langston, passed Clemens in his last outing, recording a total of 245.

Roger Clemens's performance in 1986 earned him the American League Most Valuable Player Award. Support for Clemens' selection was not unanimous, however.

He could be the best pitcher we've had here since Joe Wood.

RED SOX OFFICIAL

Everyday players cannot win the Cy Young Award, and pitchers should not be able to win the MVP award. The pitchers have their own MVP and it's the Cy Young.

HENRY AARON

I wish [Aaron] were still playing. I'd probably crack his head open to show how valuable I was.

ROGER CLEMENS

The World Series

We princes of the word-processor set had already been to work on the Curse of Babe Ruth. Whether we were inventing it, solidifying it, or exaggerating it is almost beside the point. If you talk about it, it already exists.

GEORGE VECSEY

The team with the most Cubness will lose.

CUBS FAN, QUOTED ON AN NBC WORLD SERIES BROADCAST

MVP, Almost

Bruce Hurst won two games in the 1986 World Series, including Game 5 to prevent a Mets sweep in Fenway. His performance had earned him the honor of Series MVP, according to the votes cast through Game 5. When the Red Sox failed to clinch in Game 6 and hold a 3–0 lead in Game 7, the award went to Mets third baseman Ray Knight.

After Game 6, we felt outnumbered and overwhelmed.

DON BAYLOR

I think the only thing I look back
on with regret is that I didn't
pitch in the seventh game. I was
ready to pitch.

ROGER CLEMENS

THE RED SOX FANATIC

THE FIRST SCIENTIFIC STUDY OF BASEBALL CURSES

Recent advances in social research techniques make it possible to show how, for certain baseball teams and players, calamity is so dire and so relentless that it cannot be attributed to random and impersonal misfortune alone. Using these cutting-edge tools, we have focused the refining lens of science on the conundrum of how championships are awarded, less by athleticism, than by the sinister machinery of fate. Our travails have distilled from the materials of hysteria several principles that can be defined to a reasonable scientific certainty.

Overview

Diligent research has determined that, to incur a curse, a team must either:

> 1. Commit an historically momentous trading blunder;
>
> 2. Indulge in flagitiously corrupt play, or
>
> 3. Incite the rightful damnation of a wronged fan.

An individual may also suffer a curse. It is possible for an infected player to act unknowingly, spreading pestilence as a carrier, without suffering any symptoms personally. The contaminated player may jinx one team, may jinx several teams in succession, or may transmit the infection to other individuals, particularly managers. Under the baleful influence of the curse, the sufferer will experience prolonged pennant and World Series droughts and, typically, one or more episodes of last-minute pennant-dashing catastrophe. The study has examined the fortunes of three cursed teams, one cursed player and one cursed manager. To maintain the purity of our analysis and eschew the influence of confounding effects, we have included one uncursed team in our study as a control.

Five interrelated Major League Curses have been identified. Ranked in order of virulence, they are:

1.   The Billy Goat Curse

2.   The Donkey Thomas Curse

3.   The Gene Mauch Curse

4.   The Black Sox Curse

5.   The Curse of the Bambino

Preliminary data strongly suggests that two additional, related curses may presently be developing.

The Unfriendly Confines

Of the Five Curses, the Billy Goat is, by far, the most vicious. The seeds of the menace were sewn during the Depression, and it first bore its black fruit during the dark days of World War II.

History teaches that in 1934 a Greek immigrant and Cubs fan named Vasili Sianis purchased a bar, then known as the Lincoln Tavern, in the neighborhood of Wrigley Field, Chicago. Appropriately, the check he tendered in payment for the property was drawn on insufficient funds. Sianis nonetheless made good his bargain out of the first week-end's receipts and managed to retain title to the emporium. When, some time later, a goat fell off a delivery truck traveling through the neighborhood and wandered into the bar, Sianis adopted it, gave it the name Sinovia, grew a goatee, and renamed the bar the Billy Goat Tavern.

Decades of catastrophe for an ancient and venerable franchise began when Sianis entered Wrigley Field, mascot on arm, for Game 4 of the 1945 World Series. Sinovia and escort paraded around the playing field before the game, then took their rightful places in two pricey box seats for which each held a ticket. The proximity of the seats to Cubs owner Philip Wrigley was to spell decades of doom to the darlings of the North Side. For, after some innings, Mr. Wrigley detected an unbecoming aroma emanating from the vicinity of the celebrity couple and, with Promethean bravura and folly, ordered the ejection of both man and goat. Now, one can endure injustice and hardship in silence when they are one's own, but when a harsh and dubious calumny stings a defenseless loved one, chivalry demands defiance. With tones worthy of Charlton Heston resounding down the exit ramp, Sianis decreed that the Cubs would never again win a pennant or play a World Series in Wrigley Field.

The statistical record unequivocally bears Sianis out. The Billy Goat Curse ranks first in persistence by a wide margin and is tied for number of teams affected. Anti-Positivists and other cynics who dismiss the curse as urban legend superstition ignore the primary source material.

That the Cubs have not appeared in a World Series for more than sixty years, nor captured a World Championship in nearly a century is not subject to debate. The mark of the curse is undeniable. Holding a two-games-to-one lead before the Billy Goat scandal, for example, the Cubs lost in seven games, though the last four games were played at Wrigley Field due to wartime travel restrictions. In 1969 the hard-charging Cubs wilted in August, squandering a tidy eight-and-a-half-game division lead, and yielded the postseason and an eventual World Championship to that ongoing statistical anomaly, the New York Mets.

Since the curse of Sianis, the Cubs have twice come excruciatingly close to a National League pennant. In 1984, they became only the second team to win the first two games of a five-game League Championship Series, then lose all three remaining games and, with them, a trip to the World Series. For the first team to do so, see "The Gene Mauch Curse," infra. In the final game of the NLCS, a ball rolled through the legs of Cubs first baseman Leon Durham, allowing the tying run to score and opening the floodgates for the deciding six-run San Diego inning. Cf. also, "The Curse of the Bambino," infra.

An even more bizarre fiasco struck the star-crossed franchise in 2003. The Cubs had beaten the Braves in the 2003 National League Division Series and were within eight outs of polishing off the Marlins in six games to earn a trip to the World Series. Cubs fan Steve Bartman, however, inexplicably reached above the glove of the Chicago leftfielder Moises Alou to catch a fly ball that had drifted into the front row of the stands, but remained easily within the outfielder's reach. The extra out made possible an eight-run rally and victory for the Florida upstarts. An ineffective outing by Cubs ace Kerry Wood in Game 7 doomed millions of Cubs fans to another dose of Olympian heartbreak.

Who stinks now?

VASILI SIANIS, IN A TELEGRAM TO PHILIP WRIGLEY AFTER THE
CUBS' WORLD SERIES LOSS

The Black Sox Curse

After winning two pennants in three years, the Chicago White Sox committed the unpardonable: eight of their number conspired to lose the World Series in 1919. The miscreants earned the title of Black Sox and incurred a team curse more destructive than even the legendary Curse of the Bambino. The sullied Pale Hose went pennantless for forty years and without a World Championship for eighty-eight. The franchise nearly righted itself in the Impossible Dream season of 1967. But the Curse of the Black Sox dealt a statistically anomalous hammer blow. For their last hope, South Side fans turned to the Curse of the Bambino.

The Bambino's Curse ranks among the most celebrated and most sinister misfortunes in all of sport. Before the sale of Babe Ruth to the Yankees in January 1920, the Red Sox had won five World Series without losing any, and had won four World Championships during the eight-year period preceding the sale. Thereafter, the Red Sox suffered a pennant drought of twenty-eight years and a

World Series drought of eighty-six. Not until the combined effects of two recently detected curses laid the Yankees low in 2004 could the Red Sox break free of the Bambino's kismet. But in 1967, George Herman's ghost offered no remedy for the just doom of the ChiSox. In the thick of the race with the Red Sox and two other teams until the last weekend of the season, the Chicagoans lost their final five games to the A's and Senators, teams with 184 defeats between them. The Black Sox Curse had done its worst. The Curse of the Bambino was no match for it. Only after the Babe's ire had been dissipated in 2004 could the incubus of 1919 be exorcised.

The Donkey Thomas Curse

Baseball and malaria keep coming back.

GENE MAUCH

In 1952, Pittsburgh unleashed a curse of its own. On September 2, the Pirates exercised their option to bring young slugger Frank "Donkey" Thomas to the big leagues the following year. Blessed with All-Star power and RBI totals, slugger Donkey Thomas proved to be the carrier of a black spell, which, though it left his statistics unaffected, induced overall team collapses of historic proportions three times in eleven years. The mere decision to bring Thomas up the next spring plunged the Bucs into the cellar for what seemed like permanent residence. Despite the Donkey's 102 RBIs in 1953, another 94 the next year, and respectable numbers thereafter, the Pirates languished in the basement for four straight years, suffering three years of more than 100 losses, and one of 112.

Pittsburgh snapped the streak in 1956, but only by standing on the shoulders of the Billy Goat-jinxed Cubs.

A .281 batting average, thirty-five home runs, and 109 RBIs earned Thomas a berth on the 1958 National League All-Star Team and the interest of the Reds. During the off-season, Thomas was dealt to Cincinnati as the marquee player in a six-man deal that brought Don Hoak and Harvey Haddix to Pittsburgh. A season later, the Pirates won their first pennant in thirty-three years. In one of the most improbable upsets in World Series history, Pittsburgh beat the power-laden and heavily favored Yankees, despite being outscored in the Series 55 to 27.

The Donkey's numbers in Cincinnati were disappointing, and the Reds dealt him to the Cubs after one year. A season later, the Reds won their first pennant in twenty-one years.

It was then that things began to get ugly. Thomas was to bask in the glare and glitz of the Big Apple, but not with just any New York team. In the 1961 expansion draft that gave birth to the Amazin' Mets, the New York brass concentrated on past-prime, big-name talent. They added another crepuscular slugger to their stable when they traded Gus Bell to the Braves for the Donkey in November 1961. Thomas batted cleanup for the inaugural Mets squad, belting thirty-four homers and driving in ninety-four runs. The Mets nevertheless not only finished last in the league, but set a record that still stands by losing 120 games out of 160 played, a depth of futility so profound that it completely eclipsed the pathetic Pittsburgh showing of 1953.

Thomas was to have one more chance to make history, and he took fulsome advantage of it. The Phillies of 1964 led the National League by six games with ten to go, an all but mathematically insurmountable lead. But, manager Gene Mauch decided he needed some insurance to secure the first pennant to fly over Philadelphia in fourteen years. If only the general manager had consulted his astrologer as well as his Sporting News Guide. The player the Phillies chose to lock things up was none other than Donkey Thomas. Inevitably, after the fashion of Greek tragedy, the team lost ten straight games in the season's final weeks and fell by one game to the uncursed Cardinals.

Thomas may never have suffered personally from the darkness that surrounded him, but the calamity that he spread so consistently could not be exorcised. The Donkey Thomas curse permanently infected Gene Mauch. In 1982, Mauch brought an Angels team that had won ninety-three games and the American League Western Division to the League Championship Series. Mauch's California squad quickly scored victories in the first two games of a five-game series against Milwaukee. No team had ever rebounded from such a deficit, but rebound the Brewers did. Milwaukee won the last three games and eliminated the Angels. Mauch retired.

In 1984, the Cubs won the first two games of the League Championship Series and then fell three straight times. Mauch took this as a sign that his performance in 1982 was not as ignominious as it had first seemed. But to seek reassurance from the misfortunes of a team as deeply cursed as the Cubs is to court disaster. In 1985, Mauch returned to managing. In 1986, his California Angels again won the division, exposing Mauch to another round of gut-wrenching last-minute catastrophe.

The Donkey Thomas Curse vs. The Curse of the Bambino

Oblivious to partisan allegiance, scholars rejoiced in the name of science that the Curse of the Bambino persisted into 1986. For it was from the interaction of the Babe's wrath with Gene Mauch's Donkey Thomas blight that scholars the world over gained unique insight into the hierarchy of disaster and the mechanics of doom.

In 1986, the Red Sox and Angels won their divisions. With the best record in the American League, the Red Sox were strongly favored to win the League Championship Series. Poor outings by Roger Clemens and Calvin Schiraldi, however, thrust the Angels into a three games to one lead with the fifth game scheduled for Anaheim. Angels ace Mike Witt took a 5-2 lead into the top of the ninth. The Red Sox closed the margin to one run and were twice one strike from oblivion against Angels closer Donnie Moore. The California fans were on their feet. Angels skipper Gene Mauch stood majestically in the dugout inhaling the imminence of the long-awaited rendezvous with the Autumn Classic. The California Highway Patrol ringed the field to prevent the onrush of delirious celebrants onto the diamond. But the victory never came. A two-run home run by Dave Henderson put the Red Sox ahead. The Angels tied the game in the bottom of the inning, but a Dave Henderson sacrifice fly in the eleventh inning drove the spike through California's heart, inflicting a wound from which the Angels never recovered. The Red Sox won both remaining games in Fenway Park by lopsided margins. The Bambino's wrath had been undone, his venom paling before the black fate that had haunted Gene Mauch since his brief contact with Donkey Thomas, that arch-agent of disaster, in 1964.

The Billy Goat Curse Strikes Boston

Hasty and superficial analyses have long attributed the devastating Red Sox loss in the 1986 World Series to the Curse of the Bambino. Recent research, however, has shown without cavil that the debacle was the product, not of Ruth's wraith, but of the Mother of All Curses, the Doom of Sianis. Not only had the Bambino succumbed to the Donkey that very season, but the debacle bears all the hallmarks of the Cubs' relentless curse. As one prescient Chicago rooter observed, the team with the most Cubness was destined to disaster. Not only did the Red Sox discard the title so cavalierly on a fielding gaffe identical to that which struck Leon Durham in 1984, but Bill Buckner, the author of the historic blunder, was the only former Cub on either roster! Cast not your remorse on the Sultan of Swat. Fling your fury, rather, at the odiferous consort of the Grisly Greek!

The Sign of Four, et al.

The Curse of the Bambino met its demise with the ultimate ascendancy of the Sign of Four. Throughout all of Yankee history, the fourth year of the decade has been death to New York. In 1904, their predecessors, the Highlanders sent their 41-game winner to the mound to wrest the flag from the Red Sox, only to yield the pennant on the most famous wild pitch in history. After winning three consecutive pennants in the early 1920s, the Yankees lost the flag to the Senators in 1924, the Tigers in 1934, the Browns (!) in 1944, and the Indians in 1954. Their 1964 pennant was pyrrhic poison. By taking that ill-advised flag, the Yanks suffered a pennant drought of a dozen years and the end of their forty-three-year domination of the American League. Although they mustered winners in the seventies, the Yankees succumbed to the A's in 1974 and the Tigers in 1984. A player strike prevented the flag from flying over New York, or anywhere else, in 1994. The Curse of the Bambino struck its last blow in 2003, as, the next year, the Sign of Four made the greatest comeback in sports history inevitable. It bears noting that the Yankees fell in the playoffs in 2002, only after Jason Giambi decreed that, after switching allegiance from Oakland to New York, it felt good to be in the winner's dugout. The Yankees, you may observe, have not won a World Series since they appropriated the Grape Ape from the Athletics. Could the Bronx Bombers be laboring under the influence of some insidious and invisible force? Could it be, dare I say, the Curse of the Giambino?

THE RED SOX FANATIC

FANATIC

EXORCISING THE CURSE

[W]e were afraid if the Angels won one game, we'd be in trouble. Now we had won our first game, and we felt the Yankees were in trouble.

JOHNNY DAMON

The night before, they looked like glorified batting practice pitchers. Last night the members of the Boston bullpen needed to be almost letter-perfect and for the most part, they were.

PETER MAY

There's still hope. We've still got a chance.

TIM WAKEFIELD, AFTER 2004 ALCS GAME 3

We've been right where we wanted to be. But those guys can hit and they never gave up.

DEREK JETER

All empires fall sooner or later.

LARRY LUCCHINO

You saw Varitek trying to catch it [Tim Wakefield's knuckleball]. Nobody knows where it's going to go. It's no fun trying to hit it either.

DEREK JETER

Everybody was thinking, "Well, is there some way to strap it down? Can we just screw that freakin' tendon to bone?"

THEO EPSTEIN

It [securing Curt Schilling's tendon with a screw] was totally unprecedented. It was a reasonable alternative when all else failed. And all else failed.

BILL MORGAN, RED SOX MEDICAL DIRECTOR

Mark it down. Oct. 20. It will always be the day the Sox citizens were liberated from 8 decades of torment and torture at the hands of the New York Yankees and their fans. Boston Baseball's Bastille Day.

DAN SHAUGHNESSY

Now, we don't have to go to Yankee Stadium anymore and hear those chants of "1918!"

DEREK LOWE

How many times can you honestly say you have a chance to shock the world?

KEVIN MILLAR

The Yankees created a moment 86 years in the making, a season for the ages that will forever include the 2004 Red Sox among the greatest stories in the history of American sport.

IAN O'CONNOR

Captain Courageous

Dave Roberts's steal of second in the 9th inning of ALCS Game 4 in 2004 has been justly named the most important stolen base in Red Sox history. Bill Mueller's RBI single off of Mariano Rivera to score Roberts with the tying run, and David Ortiz's twelfth-inning blast to take Game 4 have earned their place among the greatest clutch performances in any sport. But, one play that made this all possible is overlooked. In the sixth inning, the Yankees erased the first Red Sox lead of the ALCS with Hideki Matsui's triple and Bernie Williams's infield single. Jorge Posada sent Williams to second. The Red Sox were already down three games to none and couldn't hold a lead for one inning. To a sports world that considered a Red Sox collapse as inexorable as Greek tragedy, Boston was in the throes of an irresistible sweep. Jason Varitek would have none of it. An errant Mike Timlin pitch bounced away from Varitek. Bernie Williams, the Yankee runner on second base, broke for third. Varitek sprang from his crouch, pounced on the ball, and threw a bullet to third. The throw nabbed Williams. Posada scored later in the inning on an infield out. But Williams had not scored. If he had, the Red Sox would have come into the ninth inning two runs down. Neither Dave Roberts, nor Bill Mueller, nor all the king's men could have escaped a Yankee sweep.

The greatest comeback in sports history.

Period. . . . It is redemption, resilience,

retribution, and resurgence all wrapped into

one unforgettable moment.

ERIC WILBUR

I don't think anyone anywhere, no matter how drunk they were, would have said that we were going to win eight straight games.

GARY WASLEWSKI

While church bells rang in small New England towns and horns honked on the crowded streets of the Hub, the 2004 Red Sox last night won the 100th World Series, completing a four-game sweep of the Cardinals . . .

DAN SHAUGHNESSY

It was a utopian dream, the comfort of the drugged and sleeping.

The Killer B's—Babe, Bucky, Buckner, and Boone—have been Bellhorned into oblivion. Buckner just beat Mookie to the bag.

IAN O'CONNOR

Thinking they were just cutting me right to the quick, they said, "John Kerry won't be president until the Red Sox win the World Series."

JOHN KERRY

This was for Williams, Doerr and Pesky, for Yastrzemski and Yawkey, for Fisk and Rice and even Buckner and Nomar, just a few of the hundreds who suffered the pain inflicted by their New York neighbors in a rivalry that has become baseball's best.

SI.COM

This celebration is so wonderful. This is better than $1 million, better than money. This is for all the fans in Boston who suffered for so long.

JOHNNY PESKY

The citizens of the Red Sox Nation must now turn in their membership cards to Club Misery. They might be special in their zeal, but not in their misfortune. No whining allowed, when there's a parade going on.

MIKE LOPRESTI

Boston Bala who blogs in Tamil says the Red Sox finally got their "saba vimochanam" (relief from the curse).

VIJAYSREE VENKATRAMAN, *THE HINDU MAGAZINE*

If there is a guardian angel for Boston Red Sox fans (and there's some debate about that), the workload is drastically lighter today. . . . It's understandable if their stunned followers, accustomed to failure and despair aren't sure what to do next. After the hangover, that is.

DAVID LEON MOORE

I don't believe in curses. I just believe in God,

and he was the one who helped us today.

PEDRO MARTINEZ

The champagne is sitting in my hotel room cooling for the first time since 1986. I really don't care how it tastes.

KEITH LYONS

This is what we've all been waiting for. We can die happy now.

THEO EPSTEIN

Sources

Books

Gerald Aster, editor, *The Hall of Fame 50th Anniversary Book*, Upper Saddle River, New Jersey: Prentice Hall, 1988.

Baldassaro, Lawrence, editor, *The Ted Williams Reader*, New York: Simon & Schuster, 1991.

Ballew, Bill, *The Pastime in the Seventies*, Jefferson, North Carolina: McFarland, 2002.

Bess, Philip H., *Green Cathedrals*, New York: SABR, 1986.

Bjackman, Peter C., editor, *Encyclopedia of Major League Baseball Team Histories*, Westport, Connecticut: Meckler Publishing, 1991.

Boyd, Brendan C. and Harris, Fred C.,. *The Great American Baseball Card Flipping, Trading and Bubblegum Book*, New York: Tichnor & Fields, 1991.

Boyle, Tim, *The Most Valuable Players*, Jefferson, North Carolina: McFarland, 2003.

Browning, Reed, *Cy Young: A Baseball Life*, Amherst: University of Massachusetts Press, 2000.

Cataneo, David, *Tony C.* Nashville: Rutledge Hill Press, 1997.

Damon, Johnny, *Idiot*, New York: Crown Publishers, 2005.

Dickson, Paul, editor, *Baseball's Greatest Quotations*, New York: Harper Collins, 1991.

Eisen, Armand, *Play Ball*, New York: Ariel Books, 1995.

Foulds, Alan E., *Boston's Ballparks & Arenas*, Boston: Northeastern University Press, 2005.

Fusselle, Warner, *Baseball: A Laughing Matter*, St. Louis: The Sporting News, 1987.

Garner, Joe, *And the Crowd Goes Wild*, Naperville, Illinois:

Sourcebooks, Inc., 1999.

Gay, Timothy M., *Tris Speaker*, Lincoln, Nebraska: University of Nebraska Press, 2005.

Goldenbock, Peter, *Fenway*, New York: Putnam, 1992.

Halberstam, David, *Summer of '49*, New York: William Morrow, 1989.

Halberstram, David, *Teammates*, New York: Hyperion, 2003.

Hartley, Michael, *Christy Mathewson*, Jefferson, North Carolina: McFarland, 2004.

Higgins, George, V., *The Progress of the Seasons*, New York: Henry Holt and Company, 1989.

Holtzman, Jerome and Carmichael, John P., *My Greatest Day in Baseball*, Lincoln, Nebraska: University of Nebraska Press, 1996.

Honig, Donald, *American League Rookies of the Year*, New York: Bantam, 1989

Honig, Donald, *The Boston Red Sox: An Illustrated History*, Upper Saddle River, New Jersey: Prentice Hall, 1990.

James, Bill, editor, *The Great American Baseball Stat Book*, New York: Ballantine, 1987.

James, Bill, *The Historical Baseball Abstract*, New York: Villard Books, 1986.

Koppett, Leonard, *The Thinking Man's Guide to Baseball*, New York: Sports Illustrated, 2001.

LaBlanc, Michael L., editor, *Professional Sport Team Histories: Baseball*, Detroit: Gale Research, 1994.

Lautier, Jack, *Fenway Voices*, 1990, Dublin, New Hampshire: Yankee Books, 1990.

Lieb, Frederic C., *The Boston Red Sox*, New York: Putnam, 1947.

Linn, Ed, *The Great Rivalry*, New York: Tichnor & Fields, 1991.

Linn, Ed, *Hitter: The Life and Times of Ted Williams*, New York: Harcourt, Brace & Co., 1993.

Martin, George I., *Golden Boy*, Portsmouth, New Hampshire: Peter E. Randall, 2000.

McCullough, Bob, editor, *My Greatest Day in Baseball*, ed. Dallas: Taylor Publishing, 1998.

Morgan, Joe, *Long Balls, No Strikes*, New York: Random House, 1999.

Myers, Doug and Dodd, Brian, *Batting Around*, Chicago: Contemporary Books, 2000.

Nash, Bruce and Zullo, Allan, *The Baseball Hall of Shame 2*, New York: Pocket Books, 1986.

Okrent, Daniel, *Baseball Anecdotes*, New York: Oxford University Press, 1989.

Reichler, Joseph L., editor, *The World Series, 76th Anniversary Edition*, New York: Simon & Schuster, 1979.

Riley, Dan, editor, *The Red Sox Reader*, Boston: Houghton Mifflin, 1991.

Ritter, Lawrence S., *The Glory of Their Times*, New York: Harper, 1992.

Ritter, Lawrence and Honig, Donald, *The Image of Their Greatness*, New York: Crown Publishers, 1979.

Seidel,, Michael, *Ted Williams*, Lincoln, Nebraska: University of Nebraska Press, 1991.

Shaughnessy, Dan, *The Curse of the Bambino*, New York: Penguin, 2004.

Scheinin, Richard, *Field of Screams*, New York: W.W. Norton, 1994.

Shouler, Ken, *The Real 100 Best Baseball Players of All Time .. And Why*, Lenexa, Kansas: Addax Publishing Group, 1998.

Smith, Curt, *Our House: A Tribute to Fenway Park*, Indianapolis: Masters Press, 1999.

Smith, Curt, *Storied Stadiums*, New York: Carrol & Graf, 2001.

Smith, Red, *Strawberries in Winter*, New York: Quadrangle, 1974.

Smith, Robert, *World Series*, New York: Doubleday, 1967.

Smith, Ron, *The Ballpark Book*, St. Louis: Sporting News, 2003.

Sullivan, Marybeth, editor, *The Scouting Report: 1986*, New York: Harper & Row, 1986.

Wallace, Joseph, *Baseball: 100 Classic Moments in the History of the Game*, New York: DK Publishing, 2000.

Ward,, Geoffrey and Burns, Ken, *Baseball*, New York: Alfred A. Knopf, 1994.

Wilbert, Warren N., *Rookies Rated*, Jefferson, North Carolina: McFarland, 2000.

Williams, Ted, *My Turn at Bat*, New York: Simon & Schuster, 1988.

Yastrzemski, Carl, *Yaz, 1990*, New York: Doubleday, 1990.

Periodicals

Baseball Magazine

Boston American

Boston Globe

Chicago Daily Tribune

Chicago Defender

Christian Century

Christian Science Monitor

Cleveland Plain Dealer

The Hindu Magazine

London Independent

Los Angeles Times

Milwaukee Journal Sentinel

Philadelphia Enquirer

New Yorker Magazine

New York Post
New York Times
Pioneer Press
Sport Magazine
Sports Illustrated
Tufts Magazine
USA Today
Washington Post

Websites

all-baseball.com
baseball-almanac.com
baseballfever.com
baseballhalloffame.org
baseballlibrary.com
billygoattavern.com
brainyquotes.com
CNN Money.com
Diamond Angle, The
MLB.com
proquest.com
SABR.org
SI.com
thinkexist.com
wikiquote.org

Index

ABOUT THE AUTHOR

David Horne, a native of Holyoke, Massachusetts and a retired attorney, has followed the Red Sox since the days of Ted Williams, dissecting the team's every box score since the leadoff hitter was Chuck Schilling and the setup man was Tomatoes Lamabe. The father of two children and the minion of cats Merlin and Destiny, he teaches criminal justice and composition. A stalwart expatriate of the Red Sox Nation, he lives in Ohio with his wife Susan, with whom he shares passions for baseball, biking, hiking, old movies, and old music.